THE RISING

THE RISING

*Living the Mysteries of Lent,
Easter, and Pentecost*

Wendy M. Wright

UPPER
ROOM BOOKS
NASHVILLE

Except as noted,
all scripture quotations are from *Scripture Readings: Advent to Pentecost.*
Copyright ©1989 by the Carmelites of Indianapolis.
Used by permission.

All scripture quotations designated NJB
are from THE NEW JERUSALEM BIBLE, published and copyright 1985
by Darton, Longman & Todd Ltd. and Doubleday & Co., Inc., and are used
by permission of the publishers.
See page 191 for acknowledgment of copyrighted material.

Cover design: Leigh Ann Dans/Nashville
Illustration: Suzanne Harrison

ISBN 0-8358-0716-9
Library of Congress Catalog Card Number: 94-61267
Printed in the United States of America.
First printing: December 1994(5)

*To the People
of Sacred Heart Parish,
Omaha, Nebraska*

Until I am substantially oned to Him I may never have love, rest nor very bliss; that is to say, until I be so fastened unto Him that there be right naught that is made between my God and me. And who shall do this deed? In sooth, Himself, by His mercy and His grace, because He has made me for this.

Julian of Norwich
A Shewing of God's Love[1]
(Ch. 4—short text)

CONTENTS

Acknowledgments

A BOOK BASED ON THE LITURGICAL CYCLES of the Christian year owes a debt not only to the persons who had direct influence on its writing but to the wider Christian community in all its ecumenical breadth and historic depth. The liturgy carries the hope and the vision of the whole church. This book draws upon that wonderful shared richness.

More directly, gratitude is due to the editorial staff of the Upper Room (previous and present), especially Lynne Deming, who originally contracted for the book, and Robin Pippin, the manuscript's chief editor. Robert Benson acted for me once again as enspiriting presence. His creative suggestions are evident throughout. At Creighton University, I wish to acknowledge Dean Michael Lawler, whose funding made the word processing of the manuscript possible. Jackie Lynch of Omaha contributed her prompt, accurate services to that task.

Most of the scripture citations are from the inclusive language *Scripture Readings: Advent to Pentecost* (Indianapolis, Indiana: Carmelite Monastery, 1989). Otherwise *The New Jerusalem Bible* was used.

Several people were consulted in preparation for the writing. The Rev. Frank Reisinger, pastor of Lord of Love Lutheran Church, Omaha, the Rev. Carolyn Waters, pastor of Maplewood United Methodist Church, Omaha, and Dr. Russell Reno, my Episcopalian colleague at Creighton's theology department, each shared helpful insight into the theology and worship traditions of the season in their respective denominations. Dr. Eugene Selk of Creighton's philosophy department read the manuscript and provided helpful comments, and the Rev. Dennis Hamm, S.J. of the theology department was, as always, a ready and invaluable resource for questions of scriptural interpretation.

Finally, the voices and insights of all those who preach the season of the rising are heard in these pages. In particular, the homilies of the Rev. James Scholz, Sacred Heart Parish, Omaha, and the Rev. Gregory I. Carlson, S.J., as well as other members of the Jesuit community at Creighton have touched and taught me. To them I am grateful for bringing the Word to life.

INTRODUCTION

NOT ALL TIME IS THE SAME. It can be heavy enough to be a burden or so light it flies by. It is configured with peaks and valleys and long stretches of flatland between. Time can be bitter or sweet, free or constraining, endless in rapture, tedium or terror, or so elusive there never seems to be enough of it. Time, like space, has texture, density, and character.

Time's variousness is sometimes happenstance. It occurs without our intervention. But we do sometimes have a hand in shaping the contours of time.

Deep in the religious instinct of humankind there is the desire to order time so that the invisible, sacred dimension of life can be apprehended. Religious traditions the world over have created a latticework of windows in time—holy days and seasons—through which to peer into the mystery at the heart of all that is. So too have Christians from their beginnings structured time. The natural rhythms of the days, nights, and seasons become the vessels in which the sacred story of God-with-us is manifest. The drama of the life of the carpenter from Nazareth is played out on the stage of the liturgical year, as is the unfolding story of the church with its apostles, saints, and martyrs. Through this dramatic medium we are carried into the timelessness that surrounds historic time. Human and divine meet and touch. The liturgical year is the medium through which the Christian community sanctifies time—makes it holy.

Liturgical time also sanctifies those who enter into it. To venture into the movement of the church calendar is to risk transformation through the divine touch. It is to be ushered into the dynamics of incarnation, death, resurrection, and enspiriting. It is to be changed by and into the mysteries celebrated. The cyclical nature of the liturgical year in fact encourages this transformative process. Year after year we come around to the same church seasons. Year after year we experience the great feasts. Each year brings a new learning, a new changing, a new grasp of the meaning encoded in the rituals, hymns, prayers, images, and texts particular to each holy day. Each year we encounter the feasts and their mysteries at a new moment in our lives. Gradually we have the threads of our own small stories woven into the tapestry of the great stories of the faith. The layers of our lives are sewn together by the stitching of the Christian year.

There is a rich texture and density to the liturgical calendar that makes the taste of our historical moment succulent and nourishing. Our present prayers, born as they are from the limits of our individual and history-bound realities, are given depth and substance by being joined to the centuries of prayer uttered in different languages and in varied cultural expressions. Yet we pray through and in the same season, with the same symbols that continue to unfold their ancient meaning in ever new ways. The liturgical calendar is the journal that has seen recorded on its pages the aspirations and anguish of the community of the people called Christian. As we enter into its seasons we enter into the shared life of that people as it has discovered and celebrated its faith through time.

Not all Christian churches observe the church calendar in quite the same way. For highly liturgical denominations, virtually every day offers an observance of some sort. Other denominations focus on the high watermarks of the liturgical year: the great historic feasts of Christmas, Easter, and Pentecost. Either way, the calendar provides an entry into the mysteries of the faith. Time opens out to eternity for a day or a season and we find ourselves present to the reality that we celebrate.

This small book is intended to be a companion for the great liturgical season of Ash Wednesday through Pentecost, the season that surrounds the most solemn feast of the Church year, Easter. I follow here the Common Lectionary, which basically guides the Roman Catholic, Anglican (Episcopalian), Lutheran, and Methodist pattern of worship. The book is organized to conform to the structure of the season itself. Part One, The Forty Days of Lent, accompanies the reader from Ash Wednesday to the eve of Passion or Palm Sunday. It is divided into six sections that correspond to the five weeks of the Lenten season plus the half-week segment (Ash Wednesday–Saturday) at the beginning that fills out the five weeks to be a full forty days. Each of the segments is titled and deals with a theme that presented itself to me as especially significant in the scriptures designated to be read during Lent. The themes are: fasting and conversion of heart; listening and the discernment of spirits; the inversion of conventional values; forgiveness and loving our enemies; divine mothering; and the mystery of pain and brokenness.

The second part of the book is designated as Holy Week and follows the season from Palm (Passion) Sunday through the most intense and densely textured time of the entire liturgical cycle, the Triduum—Holy (Maundy) Thursday, Good Friday, and Holy Saturday.

Easter Day itself makes up a separate short segment. Its focus is, of course, the Resurrection. But the emphasis is placed upon the discovery of that event in the ordinary fabric of everyday life. It is a sort of mysticism of minutia.

The lengthy liturgical season of Easter, the Great Fifty Days, has seven brief segments corresponding to its seven weeks. The scripture readings suggested the following themes as constituent of the Easter vision—the glimpse of the reign of God—as it unfolds itself to us in all its beauty: the significance of the post-Easter appearance narratives; reconciliation; food for one another; leadership and community; the mutuality and particularity of love; the Ascension; the limits of our knowing. In each of these segments I have attended to the question of Christian community, the embodiment and fulfillment of the life, death, and resurrection of Jesus. I have done this not only by alluding to the story of the early church, whose development we trace scripturally at this time, but also by turning to historical and contemporary examples of experimental Christian community.

Pentecost, which considers both the vigil and the feast day itself, is an extended reflection on the prophetic action, the gifts and the movement of the Spirit in the community that calls itself Christian.

These meditations are not intended to be a thoroughgoing exegesis of the biblical texts. Scripture scholars much more skilled than I have written such commentaries.[2] I have tried to stay as close as possible to the Common Lectionary but, as readings change in different years, this was not always possible. Therefore, I have focused on the most representative readings, the ones that convey the variety of messages of the season most clearly. My reflections are frankly personal. Yet they draw inspiration from the wider theological and devotional life of the Christian community both in its historical and contemporary ecumenical dimensions. The reflections mix personal narrative, contemporary and historical theology, poetry, mystical exegesis, visual imagery, hymnody, devotional customs, and historic spiritual literature in the hope that readers will find something here to accompany them on many levels during this season whose richness and depth cannot be captured in a single-leveled interpretation.

The liturgical year roots our faith. It grounds the invisible, animating our lives in the visible, tactile world. It is elemental. It drapes flesh on the skeletons of our too-ghostly religiosity. It connects heaven with earth, divine with human. It allows us access to the mysteries of our faith. In its feasts and fasts we taste and see God.

THE FORTY DAYS OF LENT

This is the time of tension
between dying and birth.

T.S. ELIOT
Ash Wednesday[3]

Rend Your Hearts

It is common to think of heaven, God's place, as ordered and harmonious. Dante depicted it this way in the third book of his *Divine Comedy*. Shining, light-filled, an eternal pearl, Dante's holy spheres reflect the Divine Intelligence in their circling unity. So too Hildegard of Bingen, the twelfth century Benedictine abbess, in her visionary treatise *Scivias*, beheld the heights of heaven and in it the choirs of angels arranged in ever-widening concentric circles, mandala-like, their celestial voices raised in magnificent and mellifluous chorus.

As with heaven, so with God. Our most common imaginings about God are of peace, beauty, fullness, wholeness, completion, order, and design. By extension we often assume the spiritual life to be the same. If, however, we allow the liturgical season of Lent to carry us, we will discover that that season ushers us into a movement that is not so clearly ordered. It is most certainly not like a leisurely or even purposeful walk toward our appointed goal. The season of forty days will draw us into a movement both chaotic and creative. We enter into the rhythm of disequilibrium—indeed, of dying—essential to the formation of new life.

That God might be imagined as chaotic and creative as well as ordered and complete is perhaps not a new idea in human history, but it became quite apparent to me only a few years ago.[4] My husband, three children, and I had traveled to the Minneapolis-St. Paul area to visit friends in a religious community. As part of our entertainment, our hosts took us into the city to the Omni Theater, an educational facility attached to the Science Museum. There, in a large oval auditorium with steeply banked seats, surrounded on all sides and above by a domed projection screen, we witnessed the current natural science program. It was entitled "Ring of Fire" and documented, in a most vivid way, the activity of the volcanic range that rims the entire Pacific basin. We were visually and auditorially submerged in the hot, fiery eruptions that constitute the Pacific ring of volcanoes.

What the film presentations made very clear was that this tumultuous, destructive energy was the very energy that seethed at the core of our earth, the very energy at the root source of all earthly life. Creation itself was not ultimately stable, not orderly in some static way; rather order or temporary calm alternated with this chaotic dance of shifting energy, destruction, emergence, and upheaval. It occurred to me there, with my seven-year-old son pressed close against my arm to assure himself of some dependable, protective presence in the face of the larger-than-life spewing volcanoes that surrounded him, that if we are to allow the created world to speak analogously of the divine to us, then God as creative principal was probably as much like this tumult of flaming lava and bursting steam as God was like a lush, fruit-filled garden watered by crystal streams. And that the process of growing into God's image was as aptly pictured by the wild creativity of the ring of fire as it was by Dante's luminous globes of pearl or Hildegard's circles of celestial singers.

The forty days of Lent celebrate the dismembering, disequilibrium, and dying that are preludes to the creative transformation of Eastertide. It is a season of being changed and emptied so that new life might come to birth in us and resurrection be found in us as well.

I admit that most people do not immediately associate Lent with fiery eruptions. It is more typical to see the season as an opportunity for self-discipline or spiritual enrichment. The ancient custom of giving up things for forty days is deeply ingrained in the Christian psyche. Roman Catholics still forego little luxuries like sweets or movie-going or more pernicious luxuries like alcohol or tobacco. Eastern Orthodox Christians still observe the ancient food abstinences from meat, fish, eggs, and milk products. Further, Lent is seen as a time of seriousness. Churches of all denominations offer programs of prayer and scripture study. Wednesday soup suppers followed by prayer services are common, as are programs focused on healing. Churches may sponsor a "Talent Project," "One Great Hour of Sharing," or "Rice Bowl" collections. To deepen one's faith during Lent through study, charitable activity, or contemplative exercise is quite a common practice. These may not be activities of volcanic proportions, but their practice has much in common with the molten energy seething under the Pacific ring of fire. Both change things. And Lent is about change: of heart, of perspective, of focus, of the death that precedes new life.

Ashes to Ashes
"Even now," says our God,
    "return to me with all your heart,
with fasting and weeping and with mourning;
    rend your hearts and not your garments."
Return to the God who made you,
    for God is gracious and merciful,
slow to anger, and abounding in steadfast love.
Who knows whether we may not turn and repent,
    leaving behind us a blessing,
offerings and libations for the Most High God?
Blow the trumpet in Zion;
    sanctify a fast;
call a solemn assembly;
    gather the people.
Make holy the congregation;
    assemble the elders;
gather the children,
    even nursing infants.
Let the bridegroom leave his room,
    and the bride her chamber.
Between the vestibule and the altar
    let the ministers of the Most High, weep
and say, "Spare your people, O God,
    and make not your heritage a reproach,
    a byword among the nations.
Why should they say among the peoples,
    'Where is their God?'"
Then you, O God, became jealous for your land,
    and had pity on your people.

Joel 2:12-18

This season of change is ushered in on Ash Wednesday by a trumpet call and one of the most memorable of ritual gestures practiced by Christian communities—the imposition of ashes. Although Ash Wednesday is not an obligatory observance on the church calendar, churches are habitually filled on this day. There is something about the gesture of marking the sign of the cross on one's forehead with ashes that captures the religious imagination. It is a gesture that explicitly calls to mind our mortality. "Remember you are human" or "From dust you came, to dust you will return" are the words that traditionally accompany the signing of the cross that leaves that unmistakable black smudge on one's forehead.

The thought is sobering but not morbid. For the truth is that, considering the larger scheme of things, we live only a very short time. And the reminder of that reality can serve to put our present situation into clear perspective. It is not uncommon to read in the human interest section of the newspaper a story about a woman or man whose diagnosis of a terminal or life-threatening illness has brought about a radical change of heart. Suddenly, he or she examines priorities, sees superficial concerns for what they are, casts them aside, and determines to live each day with gratitude and fearlessness.

Ash Wednesday is such a diagnostic moment for all of us. The ritual is strikingly simple and ruthlessly egalitarian. None of us is excused from the procession. The smudgy mark does not adhere differently to man or woman, wealthy or destitute, educated or ignorant, compassionate or cruel. It labels us as one of the species, one of the mortals, who like everything else in this created universe will lose its present form. We will die. This is a certainty we share with each other. Knowledge of this radical sharing of our destiny draws us together at the onset of the season of Lent.

Sometimes the ritual of ashes takes on special significance in a given year. Two such years are tucked into my own memory and give depth and resonance to the celebration each time I observe it. The first was in the early 1970s. I was in the middle of an extended retreat in a Trappist monastery in Northern California, and my aptitude for attentiveness was brought to the fore and honed in the prayerful silence of the monastic environment. In such a milieu, spare and slow paced, gestures seem highlighted, and the ritual of Ash Wednesday stood out in high relief. There were no more than a dozen of us present: the sisters of the community, myself, and the grizzled old Belgian priest-monk who officiated at their liturgies. We formed a circle in the grey stone sanctuary with its spare zen aesthetics and its one glass wall that situated us as tiny beings surrounded by the towering redwood forests. One by one we handed around a wooden bowl containing the ashes. The person on the left marked the forehead of the person on the right with a cross. Then the one just marked turned to the right and repeated the symbolic gesture.

I knew these women. We had prayed, eaten, worked, and conversed together for weeks now. One of them turned solemnly to me, in full sight and hearing of the others, and calling me by name with the tenderness of a mother blessing her child, announced the fact of my mortality. Then I turned to another of them, spoke her name, and imprinted on her skin and mind the fact of our shared mortality. Ash Wednesday came alive for me in all its communal poignancy.

The other memorable celebration occurred when my first child was just a little girl, perhaps two or three. She was in tow as I attended an early evening service of ashes in our mission parish in Santa Barbara. The day was chilly and the old church, with its tile floors and adobe brick walls, was uncharacteristically sparsely populated. The celebrant's voice echoed down the tunnel of the nave and the gathering dusk cast deep shadows over the otherwise colorful artwork and statuary covering the walls. My daughter was demurely observant for a short while and then discovered that her own voice, as well as the celebrant's, could send thrilling echoes through the air. She began to crow in the delighted way children do when they discover some wondrous new effect of nature. Her thin soprano rang out in the gloom and chill, a bright note of vitality and newness in contrast to the somber setting and the solemn day. Just then we were called forward for the distribution of ashes. I gathered her up on my hip and moved forward but was startled when, as we moved to the front of the procession, the celebrant reached out and, parting my daughter's soft blonde bangs, marked her small forehead with the ashen sign of the cross. "Remember, you are human. From dust you came, to dust you will return." The fragility of life and its certain impermanence was suddenly painfully clear. Even this young creature, so fully alive, so much an image of promise and strength, even *she* wore the mark we all do. The poignant mystery of life with its cycles of emergence and decay, of mothers and children, of birth and death was clear.

The trumpet blast of Joel's prophecy signals the beginning of the season of change. Gather the people—all of them. We need to be alerted to the reality of the situation in which we find ourselves. We would like to live in ultimate control. We would prefer to be able to predict our futures and sketch our own life designs. But, in truth, we are merely collaborators in a larger design which is neither entirely under our control nor of our individual making.

By this, I do not mean to suggest that we should lead willy-nilly lives, buffeted about by every changing fad and circumstance. We do need to be intentional in our choices. We do need discipline, rhythm, and design to shape our work, our worship, and our relationships. What I am referring to is an ultimately very deep and existential trust in the process of life itself, a trust in the providence of God.

We live, as spiritual people, in the same way we do as biological inhabitants of this earth, most noticeably those who dwell on the rim of the Pacific ring of fire. Perched on the surface on the globe in carefully constructed protective structures, grouped in communities intended to provide us with the food, livelihood, health assistance, and nurture that we require, we proceed from day to day all too oblivious of the larger ecosystem on which we are dependent. Beneath us, with magnitude and force unimagined by us, the restive energy of created life seethes. A vast pattern of creative movement churns under our feet, interrupting and shaping the careful choreographies with which we dance our lives.

The gesture of the imposition of ashes is an invitation into the larger creative reality that undergirds our thoughtfully constructed lives. It is an invitation to change and to grow, and in the process to die to the narrowness and limitations of the familiar selves of our present making.

The Fast That I Choose

An alternate liturgical proclamation during the imposition of ashes is "Repent and live the gospel!" It gives voice to another dimension of the Lenten experience symbolized in the Ash Wednesday liturgy: repentance and the call to conversion. Although most in the Christian community today have moved away from celebrating the season in a morbidly or punitively penitential mood, it is not possible to enter into it without reflecting on our need for change and for God's mercy. We sing of that need in the words of the ancient Gregorian chant:

Kyrie eleison
Christe eleison
Kyrie eleison

Lord Have Mercy
Christ Have Mercy
Lord Have Mercy

We live in a world of both great beauty and great sorrow. We stumble along burdened by our personal limitations—our brokenness, our narrow perspectives, our fears and addictions, hatreds and suspicions. We stumble along together in a magnificent universe blighted by war, hunger, oppression, and injustice. For all our good intent and efforts, the stark reality of it is that we are not enough. And the human spirit cries out, as does the anguished voice of creation itself, Have Mercy!

The vital marshalled proclamation from the Book of Joel speaks of God's response.

> Return to me with all your heart, with fasting and
> weeping . . . for God is gracious and merciful, slow
> to anger and abounding in steadfast love.
>
> Joel 2:12-13

Mercy, almost maternal in its tenderness, reaches out to embrace us as promise and as hope. I hear this divine answer not so much as a royal pardon for the undeserving as a mother's empathic and sheltering response to the pain her children bear.

Return. Turn. Let go of the old ways that lead to such pain. Start over. Fast. Empty yourselves to be filled with something new.

Clustered together in the first days of Lent are a series of biblical readings on fasting. They vary in their message, being drawn as they are from both Old and New Testaments and from different contexts. But they all make reference to the ancient religious practice of the fast. Generally, religious fasting is a rite of ritual purification, of preparation that makes space for the holy, be it a holy day, a holy ritual, or entrance into a holy place. It also accompanies celebrations of transition or repentance. As such, it is revealed as a practice of self-denial, a conscious putting aside of the past and an embrace of or return to the ways of God. A bodily practice with inward implications, the fast has been an integral part of the Christian Lenten observance since its inception in the fourth century.

Some Christian denominations that observe Ash Wednesday still designate that day as a fast day. In the Eastern Orthodox churches the practice of fasting continues throughout the Lenten season, as it did in the past in the Roman communion (presently only Ash Wednesday and Good Friday are obligatory fasts in the Roman Catholic church). Many denominations have de-emphasized the practice of fasting in recent times.

But remnants of it may remain, for example, in a Shrove Tuesday (the day before Ash Wednesday) pancake dinner, a dinner originally instituted to use up household fats and sweets forbidden in the Lenten fast.

The Lenten fast takes its gospel inspiration from the account of the forty-day fast Jesus undertook after his baptism by John in the river Jordan. According to the Synoptic Gospels of Matthew, Mark, and Luke, he was led into the wilderness by the Spirit that he had received in his baptismal initiation. The fast also draws upon the ascetic inheritance from the desert monastic tradition as well as the ritual inheritance from Judaism.

Christian fasting through the centuries has been understood in various ways. One long-lived interpretation sees the fast as a way to strengthen the spiritual life by weakening the attractions of sensory pleasures. John Climacus, seventh-century abbot of a monastic community on Mount Sinai and the author of *The Ladder of Divine Ascent*, a treatise on the ascetical-spiritual life (and the most widely read piece of spiritual literature in the eastern Christian world), makes this point in his vivid prose. Like many of his contemporaries, John believed that subduing the passions, including the bodily appetites, was necessary to spiritual maturation. Dispassion, or *apathaeia*, was the goal of spiritual discipline. Chief among the bodily passions, gluttony, came in for stern criticism. Its antidote, fasting, not only reversed the evil of gluttony but opened the door for a host of other spiritual benefits.

> Control your appetites before
> they control you. . . . For the truth
> is, as one will discover, that the
> belly is the cause of all human
> shipwreck. . . .
> [To fast] is to do away with
> whatever pleases the palate. Fasting
> ends lust, roots out bad thoughts, frees
> one from evil dreams. Fasting makes for
> purity of prayer, an enlightened soul, a
> watchful mind, a deliverance from blindness.
> Fasting is the door of compunction, humble
> sighing, joyful contrition, and end to
> chatter, an occasion for silence, a custodian
> of obedience, a lightening of sleep, health

> of the body, an agent of dispassion, a
> remission of sins, the gate, indeed, the
> delight of Paradise.[5]

Although this perspective still lingers in the Lenten air, we tend to think of fasting as something done by others more fervid or disciplined than we. In the contemporary world we are more apt to think of it as either a health practice or a technique for social and political protest. In the first case, although often simply utilized as a medical procedure (as before surgery), fasting is still often seen as a method of purification, sometimes with spiritual benefits, a sort of cleansing of the interconnected network of body, mind, and spirit. In the same way, the use of fasting as social protest often has a distinctly religious dimension, which distinguishes it from the hunger strike undertaken without religious motivation. Mahatma Gandhi, the spiritual architect of Indian independence from British colonial rule, used fasting as a technique to bring about social change. Abstinence from food was one aspect of his theory of nonviolent resistance. Gandhi was convinced that violent response to injustice only perpetrated more violence. He chose instead to respond to oppression by orchestrating large-scale actions of resistance that finally forced the British to withdraw from the Indian subcontinent. Among his methods, and high on the scale of his moral statements, was his campaign of fasting. At a critical moment in the resistance, when deep-seated ethnic tensions and frustration with the slow progress of independence erupted in mob violence between Hindu and Muslim citizens, Gandhi undertook a dramatic personal fast. So great was his authority and so beloved was he by most of the Indian people, that his public refusal to eat, even though it result in his death, finally persuaded the mobs to curb their violence.

Dramatic actions such as the nonviolent fast have much in common with the bizarre, theatrical gestures of the biblical prophets. Zechariah recounted how he ate the scroll of prophecy he was given to deliver to the Israelites; Ezekiel shaved his head, carried baggage on his shoulders, lay on one side for a protracted period of time, and danced with a sword over a mock city. Jeremiah set up a clay city and smashed it. Each of them performed these shocking actions as part of their ministry of conversion, getting people to take notice. This sort of guerilla theater on behalf of

God's prophetic message was similarly practiced by Jesus when he strode into the temple and overturned the tables of the moneychangers.

The extension of fasting beyond a discipline of personal conversion to include the conversion of society has deep biblical rooting. Among the passages read during the early days of Lent is a robust warning issued by the prophet Isaiah.

> Cry aloud, spare not,
>   lift up your voice like a trumpet;
> declare to my people their transgression,
>   to the house of Jacob their sins.
> Yet they seek me daily,
>   and delight to know my ways,
> as if they were a nation that did justice
>   and did not forsake the ordinance of their God;
> they ask of me righteous judgments,
>   they delight to draw near to God.
> 'Why have we fasted and you do not see?
> Why have we humbled ourselves, and you take no note of
>   it?'
> Behold, in the day of your fast you seek your own pleasure,
>   and oppress all your workers.
> Behold, you fast only to quarrel and to fight
>   and to hit with wicked fist.
> Fasting like yours this day
>   will not make your voice to be heard on high,
> Is such the fast that I choose,
>   a day for people to humble themselves?
> Is it to bow down their heads like rushes,
>   and to spread sackcloth and ashes under them?
> Will you call this a fast,
>   and a day acceptable to your God?
> Is not this the fast that I choose:
>   to loose the bonds of injustice,
>   to undo the thongs of the yoke,
>   to let the oppressed go free,
>   and to break every yoke?
> Is it not to share your bread with the hungry,
>   And bring the homeless poor into your house,
> When you see the naked, to cover them,
>   and not to hide yourself from your own family?

> Then shall your light break forth like the dawn
>   and your wounds shall quickly be healed;
> Your righteousness shall go before you, the glory of God
>   shall be your rear guard.
> Then you shall call, and God will answer,
>   you shall cry, and God will say,
>   Here I am.
>
> Isaiah 58:1-9

So too in the twentieth century, religious protestors against evils they consider to be a defamation of God's creation—nuclear arms, ecological pollution, and such—have used techniques of nonviolent resistance to draw public attention to the moral dimensions of these issues. Fasting has been among these techniques. Recently, Katherine Dunham, a Haitian-American woman famed for her artistry in the dance, launched a public fast to quicken the American conscience about the impoverished nation to the south. And the late Cesar Chavez, champion of the migrant farm workers in California, likewise merged the ancient practice of fasting with his religious concern for the economic and social plight of the poor.

The proclamation of a fast at the outset of the season of Lent thus has many dimensions. It is a call to continuing conversion or turning, a call to reorient, reassess, and rearrange our lives to more fully respond to God's invitation. The call is at once profoundly personal and uncompromisingly communal. It is a call to enter into a liminal season, a season of dying before being born, a season of creative chaos and upheaval, a season whose purpose is to knit us closer to our God.

Led into the Wilderness

Since the fifth century the Christian community in the west has elected on the First Sunday of Lent to hear proclaimed the story of Jesus' temptation in the wilderness. The account appears in Matthew, Mark, and Luke in variant forms. It is at the same time a recounting of a seminal initiatory event in the life of Christ and an archetypal image of part of the process of our own Lenten dying—the encounter with spirits in the wilderness. It depicts Jesus being led into the wild lands where demonic forces emerge. Yet he is led there by the Spirit bestowed on him at baptism. God's creative energy draws him into an intense experience of discernment. He is lured, through the devil's invitation, to accept a vision of himself and his life that in the end cannot define him as the chosen one that he is.

Jesus was led up by the Spirit into the wilderness to be tempted by the devil. And he fasted forty days and forty nights, and afterward he was hungry. And the tempter came and said to him, "If you are the Chosen One of God, command these stones to become loaves of bread." But Jesus answered, "It is written,
    'You shall not live by bread alone, but by every
    word that proceeds from the mouth of God.'"
Then the devil took him to the holy city, and set him on the pinnacle of the temple, and said to him, "If you are the Chosen One of God, throw yourself down; for it is written,
    'I will give my angels charge of you,'
    'On their hands they will bear you up, lest you
    strike your foot against a stone.'"
Jesus said to the devil, "Again it is written, 'You shall not tempt the Most High God.'" Again, the devil took him to a very high mountain, and showed him all the realms of the world and the glory of them, and said, "All these I will give you, if you will fall down and worship me." The Jesus said: "Begone, Satan! for it is written,
    'You shall worship the Most High God
    and God only shall you serve.'"
Then the devil left him, and behold, angels came and ministered to him.

Matthew 4:1-11

Visual artists over the centuries have tried to capture one or another of the moments of encounter between the devil and Jesus portrayed in this gospel. Duccio di Buoninsegne, the late thirteenth century Italian Renaissance painter, depicted the third of Matthew's temptations on the lower panels of his altarpiece painted for the Cathedral in Siena. Dominating the picture is a larger-than-life Jesus perched on the top of a stony knoll, captured at the moment when he makes a definitive rejection of Satan. His right hand is outstretched in a gesture of defiance toward the retreating devil. His left hand pulls his cloak closely about him as if to protect himself from the tempter's evil. Huddled behind Jesus are two angels waiting to minister to the triumphant Lord. At the angels' feet, below the knoll and ascending the hilly terrain, are miniature walled cities, with their turrets and spires aloft. The satanic figure, also more than lifesize, is shown retreating the knoll, cowed by Jesus' firm gesture of renunciation. Duccio paints the devil as the fallen angel he is, a sinister figure with great bat wings, his scowling satyr-like face turned back in a sneer at his triumphant foe.

The temptation in the wilderness deserves not only to be heard in the polite way it often is during church services. It deserves to be graphically imaged as it was by artists like Duccio or dramatically imaged by us in prayer. In this way a gospel passage can unfold and become more than a history lesson or a moral cautionary tale. It can become a living text that speaks creatively to our own lives.

As is suggested by its fifteen centuries of liturgical prominence, this wilderness drama has been speaking creatively to Christians for most of our history. I see in it a tale of discernment, of wrestling with different spirits or voices heard in the self, the process of which can help us to sift through the variety of motives, impulses, and values that guide our choices. But discernment is not simply about making choices, right from wrong, better from worse. It is also about self-knowledge, coming to know the constellation of one's own particular gifts and limitations. Discernment is about coming to some clarity about what moves us. It involves attending to the results of the actions occasioned by our motivations.

In this first week of Lent we are asked to venture into the wilderness of our own hearts and there listen to the many voices that beckon us in one direction or another. What are the sources of this multitude of voices?

How do we tell the texture or quality of one from another? How do we choose which voices we should follow? What is the sound of the voice of God perceived there?

The Standard of Christ

One of the most famous and influential persons who spent time engaging the account of the temptations, as well as the rest of the Gospel narratives, was Ignatius Loyola, sixteenth-century Spanish founder of the Society of Jesus (the Jesuits). Following his own dramatic conversion and a lengthy period in which he re-evaluated and altered his life to conform to what he believed was the gospel imperative, Ignatius wrote a little guide book, *The Spiritual Exercises*, for praying people who wanted to know and follow Jesus more closely. At the core of *The Spiritual Exercises* is the practice of affective meditation on the life and passion of Christ (systematic yet imaginative and heartfelt prayer focused on the Gospels). These biblical meditations gave rise in Ignatius to other meditations based on gospel precepts. Engaging in the Exercises is a method of spiritual formation, of dying to old ways and perspectives and being born to ones that are new. One of Ignatius's meditations is called "The Two Standards" and introduces the exertant (the one undergoing the Exercises) into the contrasting realities ruled over by Christ and Satan. Ignatius has the exertant, with the help of a spiritual guide, imagine as vividly as possible

> a great plain composing the whole region about Jerusalem, where the sovereign Commander-in-Chief of all the good is Christ our Lord; and another plain about the region of Babylon, where the chief of the enemy is Lucifer.[6]

Through the guide, Ignatius proceeds to lead the exertant through a meditation first on Satan's presence, which inspires terror and horror, and then on the presence of Christ, whom he depicts as beautiful and attractive. At the core of the two reflections are addresses the two commanders make to their troops. Satan encourages his demons to promote his own standard.

> He goads them on to lay snares for men. . . . First they are to tempt them to covet riches . . . that they may the more easily attain the empty honors of this world, and then come to overweening pride.[7]

Christ admonishes his companions in battle to

> Help all, first by attracting them to the highest spiritual poverty . . .
> even to actual poverty. . . . they should lead them to a desire for
> insults and contempt, for from these springs humility."[8]

What Ignatius does in this extended reflection is characterize the primary virtues of the Christian life as it had developed in his day and contrast them with their opposites. Poverty, contempt, and humility emerge in opposition to riches, honor, and pride. This later triumvirate were certainly the temptations of a man of Ignatius' time and social standing, a nobleman of Spain in the sixteenth century. And the virtues of the Christ life—poverty, contempt, and humility—were those virtues that the cumulative tradition of spirituality had generally held up as exemplary.

Loyola's enumeration of the quality of the Christian life and what opposes it certainly draws inspiration from the scriptural narrative of Jesus' temptation in the wilderness. There Satan entices him with food (material rather than spiritual), encourages him to use his close relation with God, and offers him power over the world. In short, Jesus is tempted with riches, pride, and honor. He chooses instead a life defined otherwise, by other values and virtues.

Odd virtues they were—poverty, contempt, and humility. But they speak, I think (with some careful attention to translation for the contemporary world), with continuing power. I know it is not popular to hold up virtues like these three in today's America. There are good reasons for this. We hold dear the hope that all people should enjoy the opportunity to live peaceful, free, and prosperous lives. We tend to equate poverty with lack of opportunity. We tend to see contempt as exclusionary prejudice and humility as the self-deprecation that cripples people from taking their rightful place in the good society. I would suggest that harsh economic depravation, unjust vilification by others, and self-hatred are hardly goals of the spiritual life.

But I also think that this triumvirate of qualities can be viewed in a different light. Poverty might be creatively understood as a preference for simplicity and a desire for inner spaciousness. To unburden ourselves of the acquisitions that clutter both our outer and inner lives can leave us free to respond to God and others more readily. Contempt might be interpreted as an opportunity to relocate our sense of self-validation from the outer to the inner realm. We come to ask: "Who do I say I am?" and "Who does God say I am?" rather than allowing others to answer those questions for us. Humility is best seen, I think, as the recognition of our simultaneous blessedness and brokenness. We are called to enormous potential as children of God, yet each of us is starkly limited. True humility is the clear-eyed recognition of our simultaneously blessed and broken identity.

Here I tread carefully, for it seems to me that the Christian life can too often masquerade as poor, humble, and selfless when underneath self-righteousness, subtle manipulation of others, or resentment stew. I would also suggest that poverty, contempt, and humility are not necessarily universally applicable spiritual values. In relationships of abuse or under conditions of oppression, to cultivate such qualities may be to choose not the standard of Christ but the standard of Satan that would affirm the status quo.

What I find challenging about Jesus' elevation of poverty, contempt, and humility is that they reverse the accepted values of the normative society. They stand things on their heads. They suggest that this kingdom that Jesus has been proclaiming is not something that we have captured in the ways we habitually do things now. What that reversal is about and how the virtues of the standard of Christ are lived is a theme that will continue to unfold scripturally in the liturgy of Lent. Suffice it to say now that, in our wilderness encounter, we are introduced to the notion of reversal and surprise.

We are also introduced to the idea that the way things are now, the standards by which we generally judge and choose, for all their glamour and attraction, are underneath brooding and sinister. Something is awry. The odor of evil clings to the riches, power, and honor that draw us so readily. However one accounts for the presence of evil in the world (and it is not necessary to posit that there are intelligent forces directing evil), we recognize that profound evil does exist, in our institutions, in our social lives, in our personal interactions, in the potentialities of our own hearts. A wise spiritual director friend of mine says it well, "We are all capable of all of it."

We are constantly confronted with choices that involve our discernment. Often the shadowy lure of evil is obvious in the choice, sometimes it is not. Often, our complicity in evil has most to do with our passive acquiescence to the cultural evil that surround us—the evils of racism, sexism, hunger, poverty, violence, and such. Lent is a time to reflect on the temptation we all face to simply accept the status quo, to ignore the hard questions facing us. What does it mean to follow? What does it mean to enter into the wilderness and choose to know ourselves and each other as beloved daughters and sons of God?

Desert Listening

Several years ago I was invited to give a Lenten retreat in Wyoming at a thriving university campus Catholic parish. The parish ministers had gone to great lengths to make the Lenten season come alive for their parishioners. Worship services were carefully designed to heighten the Lenten mood. Visually, the church interior proclaimed the seasonal mood. Banners of the traditional Lenten purple (the liturgical color of penance) hung from the ceiling of the church. There were also large earthenware bowls filled with sand decorating the steps leading to the altar. While this in itself is not unusual in denominations that are highly liturgical, this parish high in the mountainous plains of Wyoming had at least one visual and tactile sign of the season that was unique. They had filled the holy water fonts that stand at the doorways to the church with desert sand. Entering the sanctuary it is customary to dip one's fingers in the water and make the sign of the cross. During this year's season that habituated gesture would be arrested in process. One would find one had dipped into the dryness of sand.

By this hand-dipping gesture I was made keenly aware of the Lenten desert invitation. I was taken back not only to Jesus' wilderness drama but also to the desert ascetics of fourth century Egypt, Palestine, and Syria. For me they are models of discernment. These zealous Christians, convinced that discipleship meant a radical transformation of life, left the "world" with its false values and fled to the desert, there to do battle with the "worldly" demons lodged in their own hearts. Pride, greed, self-aggrandizement, lust for power—all the false motivations that drive human beings—were ferreted out and replaced by the spirit of Christ: the spirit of compassion, humility, and purity of heart.

The key to the transformation of the desert was the ascetic's listening ear. In silence and solitude they cultivated a hearing attuned to catch the voice of God. They learned that going apart from the noisy environment of daily life to the silence of the desert enabled them to perceive deeper levels of noise and silence. In the desert's quiet they discovered the noisiness within, the restless cacophony of voices raging in their hearts. Yet if they persevered further, they found that beneath that was another level of silence, an abyss of stillness that encompassed all that exists. There, in the primal silence within the human heart, the voice of God could be clearly heard.

The patient process of untangling the threads of voices, of settling down to the center was the lifelong work of the desert. It is our work as well. Like the desert ascetics, we must learn the art of inner listening. Where do the many voices within come from? And where do they lead? To self-aggrandizement and judgment of others, or to compassion and reconciliation? Which of the voices is the voice of God? To what am I called? What is God's invitation for me at this season of my life?

Lent is a time for tuning our ears, for listening carefully, for discerning the texture and quality of our own demons, for attending to God's unceasing, creative plea amidst the noise of cultural pressures, the busyness of life, and our own self-limiting habits. Some of our Lenten discernments may be fairly straightforward. We may have become inattentive in our eating or drinking and need to give our oversatiated bodies a holiday. We may need to curb a smoking habit that endangers the health of those we live with as well as ourselves. We may need to cultivate a more rhythmic pattern of prayer or bring the scriptures into clearer focus in our everyday life. We may need to mend the pieces of a broken relationship. We may need to take some of the time we hoard so tightly for work and lavish it on our children or friends. We may be called to respond to the cry of the poor, to feed the hungry, to shelter the homeless, or to visit the prisoner. All these can rightly be discerned as God's prompting to a freer life.

But the ongoing process of discernment, which I think is the more subtle invitation of the Lenten season, is not always so straightforward. It involves a radical and risky self-evaluation and a commitment to rethink and rework everything you know and are. God is always calling us out of ourselves, into a more generous freedom, so that we can love and serve ourselves and one another more authentically.

What does that freedom look like for each of us this season? We might have images in our minds as to what we ideally should be. But perhaps sometimes the ideal is less important than the real. The spiritual life is not a generic undertaking, despite the fact that it is often characterized as such. Rather, it involves the unique encounter of a particular woman or man in her or his concrete history and circumstance with the God who dared and continues to dare to be incarnate in human form. The spiritual life is never twice the same. Always utterly new, always surprising, the human meeting with God through the discernment of spirits invites us to become listeners to God's voice heard among the multitude of voices crowding the human heart. We must be open to hear the surprising message it may bring.

The Will of God

Frequently I am asked by people eager to pursue a spiritual life the question, "How do I know the will of God?" The historic literature is insistent that this pursuit is to be the objective in our discernment. To know and follow God's will brings us to fullness of life. But how do we know what that will is?

In response to the query, I often share a story. When I was a fairly new graduate student beginning my studies in the history of Christian spirituality, I was invited to give a day of Lenten reflection for a group of church women at a retreat center in Northern California. The talk was to be part of a series entitled "Women of Wisdom," which was meant to make available to twentieth-century women of faith the fruits of prayer ripened on the vines of earlier women's lives. St. Jane de Chantal, the subject of the dissertation on which I was embarking, was to be one of the wise women highlighted in the series. I came to the retreat center clothed in the somewhat superior air of cloistered graduate students, especially those engaged in the study of weighty subjects.

The group consisted of about fifty mid-life women, most of whose talents had been utilized in making a home for husbands and children. Although few had access to the intellectual resources that I had in graduate school, they were well trained in the deep prayer that thrives, by necessity, in the disciplines of familied life. I had in store for them a set of conferences on St. Jane to be alternated with a series of silent times of reflection. I wanted it to be a very deep and solemn and spiritual experience.

But there was one woman who irked me more and more as the day went on. She did not fit my notion of someone who should be on a prayer retreat. For one thing, she was loud—in her demeanor, her dress, her voice. Whenever we ended one of our conferences and I instructed us to move silently into the depths of our hearts, she would inevitably begin to talk and laugh raucously. She was overweight, wore tasteless clothing, and chain-smoked. She, of course, was to become the instrument of my own instruction. During the lunch break I wandered into the retreat center bookstore. On sale was a copy of an Anthology of Western Mysticism that I had recently edited in collaboration with one of my professors. We had had nothing to do with choosing the cover design for the book; the publisher had seen to that. When it had arrived I gave it little thought. A flower of some sort on a blue background—I did not stop to wonder at the choice. The loud woman was also browsing in the store and she caught sight of me. "What a wonderful cover!" she declared. "Hens and Chickens!" I was nonplussed. Then it began to dawn on me. The flower which I had inattentively seen as generic was in fact the desert plant known as Hens and Chickens, a fat desert succulent that stays bloomless for long periods then, in a mad display of prodigal fecundity, produces one extravagant blossom. How apt for a book on mysticism, that hidden life born of the desert wilderness tradition that speaks of the voluptuous union of the soul and God. This woman who didn't belong at my day of prayer knew more about the cryptic symbol on the front of my book than did I.

She confounded me more and more during the course of the day with her deep, incisive comments, always in that strident voice that grated and always accompanied by those awkward, ungenteel movements. Her final teaching gift came to me at the end of the day when she approached me and announced that she had spent years asking holy people the answer to the question, "How do you know the will of God?" She was never satisfied until recently. She wanted to share with me what one man had suggested to her. If you think you sense the will of God in your life in some long-range, highly detailed plan, something you can see stretching out with clear goals and successes into the future, *that* is *not* the will of God. If, however, you have an insistent sense that the next, very hesitant step beyond which you can see nothing is in fact the step that must be taken, *that* is most likely the will of God for you.

What are we assuming when we ask to know God's will? Are we

imagining a God who, like a master planner, has a five-year, ten-year, or lifetime plan mapped out for us and leaves it up to us to figure out what it is? Do we harbor such a deterministic notion of divinity? Are our discernments basically concerned with "getting it right," with making the choice that down the road we will be able clearly to see was "correct" because everything came out in the end in a neatly wrapped, manageable package? Do we live with this sort of tidy, self-protective, predictable kind of God?

I prefer to rephrase the question and thus to reframe the reference somewhat. I ask instead, "What is God's longing for our lives?" Such reframing will situate us in the arms of a God who desires the fulfillment of creation, who longs for justice, mercy, and love to dwell among the creatures and the created world fashioned in the divine image and likeness. We are unique, unrepeatable, loving responses to the divine desire. There is a particularity to our reciprocal desiring. But the path of love that I walk is neither predetermined nor clear-cut. It is forged in the process of walking day by day, listening deeply to the silence brooding beneath the noisy instructions issuing from without and within our own hearts. God's will is not a puzzle to be solved but a mystery to be lived into. It is a mystery whose contours emerge as we journey on.

One of the pieces of our Lenten journey is cultivating the art of discernment, listening for the voice of God in the wilderness of our hearts, trying to sense the divine will. Discernment is part of our ongoing conversion, our ongoing struggle with the holy mystery and creative chaos that we encounter as we turn toward the rising beacon of the light of Christ.

The Last Shall Be First

In her short story "Revelation," Flannery O'Connor, the fiction writer famous for her pungent characterizations of southern life, drew a portrait of one Ruby Turpin, a "respectable, hardworking, church-going woman." Mrs. Turpin was an individual concerned with the classes of people— (beginning at the lowest rung) niggers, white trash, home owners, home-and-land owners. She prided herself that she and hers were not trashy and lazy and unrespectable like those in the lower classes. The proud owner, with her husband Claud, of a clean pig-parlour and a well-run farm, Mrs. Turpin was grateful to Jesus for who and what she was. The story recounts how her tidy world was shattered when she was attacked, verbally and physically, by an unbalanced young woman in a doctor's waiting room. Her smug and tightly knit assumptions about the identity of righteousness and respectability were thrown into question by the girl's unflattering characterization of her. Surely the other waiting room occupants, so clearly of lesser quality than she, should better have been singled out. As she brooded in anger over the incident while hosing down her swine, Mrs. Turpin was the recipient of a vision with gospel overtones.

> Until the sun slipped finally behind the tree line, Mrs. Turpin remained there where her gaze bent to them as if she were absorbing some abysmal life-giving knowledge. At last she lifted her head. There was only a purple streak in the sky, cutting through a field of crimson and leading, like an extension of the highway, into the descending dusk. She raised her hands from the side of the pen in a gesture hieratic and profound. A visionary light settled in her eyes. She saw the streak as a vast swinging bridge extending upward from the earth through a field of living fire. Upon it a vast horde of souls were rumbling toward heaven. There were whole companies of white trash, clean for the first time in their lives, and bands of black niggers in white robes, and battalions of freaks and lunatics shouting and clapping and leaping like frogs. And bringing up the end of the procession was a tribe of people whom she recognized at once as those who, like herself and Claud, had always had a little of everything and the God-given wit to use it right. She leaned forward to observe them closer. They were marching behind the others with

great dignity, accountable as they had always been for good order and common sense and respectable behavior. They alone were on key. Yet she could see by their shocked and altered faces that even their virtues were being burned away. She lowered her hands and gripped the rail of the hog pen, her eyes small but fixed unblinkingly on what lay ahead. In a moment the vision faded but she remained where she was, immobile.

At length she got down and turned off the faucet and made her slow way on the darkening path to the house. In the woods around her the invisible cricket choruses had struck up, but what she heard were the voices of the souls climbing upward into the starry field and shouting hallelujah.[9]

The daily scripture readings for the second week of Lent play with this same sort of shocking reversal of conventional wisdom. Over and over the theme asserts itself: the last shall be first. The mother of Zebedee's sons petitions Jesus that her boys might sit at his right hand in his realm, but Jesus retorts that whoever would be great among them must be one who serves (Matt. 20:17-28). Upbraiding the scribes and Pharisees for attracting attention to their piety, Jesus tells his followers that they should not allow themselves to claim the distinction of titles like rabbi or teacher. Instead, the greatest among them must be servant. Moreover, anyone who exalts himself will be humbled and anyone who humbles himself will be exalted (Matt. 23:1-23). The poor man Lazarus, doomed in life to begging at the gates of the rich man's house, is carried away at death to the bosom of Abraham while the wealthy man ends up in the torments of Hades (Luke 16:19-31). The righteous among the people of Israel are warned in parable form that the kingdom of God will be taken from them and given to people who will produce its fruits. Referring to himself, Jesus says that the stone that the builders rejected will become the cornerstone, thus underscoring the significance of that which is cast off and overlooked (Matt. 21:33-46).

In the kingdom that Christ proclaims everything is topsy-turvy. This is made abundantly clear at the onset of the season when Jesus, in his wilderness temptation, is offered everything that is ordinarily valued and pursued. It is not simply godless people who have their heads turned by the respect of others, lovely possessions, and positions of importance. We all do. Each in our own sphere. Yet we are invited into a different valuation of ourselves. We are important because we are God's beloved ones, not because we possess great wealth, are held in esteem by others, or wield power and influence.

Upside-Down Gospel

One of my favorite interpreters of the wisdom that the last shall be first is Francis de Sales, seventeenth-century bishop and spiritual writer. Bishop de Sales made the topsy-turvy vision of kingdom reversal the cornerstone of his teaching. His approach focuses on the pursuit of virtue, formation of character we might call it today, and involves the cultivation of culturally undervalued personal qualities. Not only did he preach a preference for spiritual poverty, humility, and contempt, as did his predecessor Ignatius Loyola (Francis was, in fact, a product of Ignatian education and *The Spiritual Exercises*), he went so far as to sing the praises of a host of "little virtues." Many of his contemporaries preached of virtue, especially great, heroic virtues like courage or exemplary self-discipline. Francis urged his followers to develop instead the little, hidden virtues like gentleness, kindness, patience, simplicity, and mutual regard—the interpersonal virtues. These were for him the qualities of the Christ life.

De Sales drew his portrait of the gentle Jesus from the Gospel of Matthew (11:29-30), in which Christ is quoted as inviting others to take his yoke upon their shoulders, to come and *learn* from him, for he is gentle and humble of heart. For de Sales this learning was to be acquired by imitating Jesus' own gentleness and humility. Not merely "nice" acceptable virtues, the little virtues held the keys to the kingdom. For by cultivating them one subverted the dominant character values held in esteem by most.

Chief among de Sales' "little virtues" is *douceur*, often rendered in English as gentleness, sweetness, graciousness, meekness, and the like. *Douceur* is the quality of person that corresponds to the light burden offered by the Matthean Jesus to those otherwise heavy-laden. It connotes an almost maternal quality of service, a quality of service bathed in tender concern. *Douceur* also suggests a sense of being grace-filled, graceful in the broadest sense of the term. This gracefulness extends from external behavior—pleasant manners and convivial disposition—to the quality of a person's heart, the way one is ordered and disposed interiorly. *Douceur* is ideally exhibited in all situations, even the most difficult, and underlies one's every act.

For Bishop de Sales, the person who can preserve gentleness

(*douceur*) in the midst of sorrows and sufferings and peace in the midst of multiplicity and busyness of affairs is a person who is almost perfect. Gentleness was for him eschatologically significant. It is a sign of the kingdom that Jesus preached. The invitation is to come and learn from him. And what is Jesus like? He is gentle and humble of heart. That is, his most essential self, the point from which all thought and action flow—the heart—has the qualities of gentleness and humility. For de Sales this was a radically countercultural idea, for most hearts are not gentle and humble but proud, grasping, and envious. There is thus a subtle subversiveness to this teaching of the Christ life. De Sales was quoted as saying, "Nothing is so strong as gentleness, nothing so gentle as real strength." To live the reversal dynamic of the kingdom was to live the little virtues and begin to realize God's intent for humankind. All of the little virtues are relational. They offer the possibility of realizing a community of mutual respect and love. What was envisioned was very biblical, the creation of a human community that loved as it had first been loved by God.

The Voices of the Last

Francis de Sales saw the cultivation of the little virtues as a response to the gospel. In today's Christian community the gospel imperative that the last shall be first is most visibly expressed in the social sphere. The twentieth century has witnessed the ascendancy of the social gospel in mainline Protestant denominations and the systematic articulation of a theological tradition of social ethics in Roman Catholicism.[10] The gospel reversal insight has taken the form of social analysis. Where injustice, oppression, hunger, and violence exist and the diminution of the innate dignity of the human person occurs, there must be the focus of our attention. God's concern and, by extension, our concern, is to be directed toward those who are last and least. The outcast, the prisoner, the poor, the homeless, victims of abuse and injustice, those discriminated against because of race or gender—these are among those whom we are called to put first. They are not to be the objects of our charity but the beneficiaries of justice.

Perhaps the imperative to address social issues through gospel eyes has recently been seen most dramatically in the Latin American churches. Christians south of the U.S. border survive in a social reality much harsher than our own. The vast chasms of economic inequity between rich and poor are highly visible, the devastating effects of military dictatorships are gruesomely carved in the flesh of political opponents, and the legacy of colonial oppression is etched deeply into the constant social unrest. The brutality of torture, disappearance, and intimidation can be keenly seen in the policies of many governments. In this climate, Christian communities have increasingly taken on the mantle of advocacy on behalf of the poor and oppressed. They have developed a theology that focuses on the liberating power of the Christian message.

Forming "base communities" (local faith-sharing groups), catechists (religious educators) have encouraged their flocks to reflect on their own experience in light of the gospel message. In the 1970s, base communities were formed in Solentiname, Nicaragua. Faith conversations of the membership, mostly illiterate peasants, in concert with their catechist Ernesto, have been recorded. In this conversation about the story of the rich man and the beggar Lazarus who sits outside his door (Luke 16:19-31), they bring a focused sense of the gospel truth that the last shall be first as it is manifest in their own social reality.

> FELIPE: "I think the poor man here stands for all the poor, and the rich man for all the rich. The poor man is saved and the rich man is damned. That's the story, a very simple one, that Jesus tells us."

> GLORIA: "The rich man's sin was that he had no compassion. Poverty was at his door, and that didn't disturb him at his parties."

> WILLIAM: "The traditional interpretation of this passage is wrong and is used for exploitation; because the poor man has been led to believe that he must patiently endure because after death he's going to be better off and that the rich will get their punishment."

> FELIPE: "As I see it, this passage was rather to threaten the rich so they wouldn't go on exploiting; but it seems it turned out the opposite: it served to pacify the people."

> OLIVIA: "I think the word of God has been very badly preached, and the church is much to blame in this. It's because the Gospel hasn't been well preached that we have a society still divided between rich and poor. There are few places like Solentiname, where the Gospel is preached and we understand it. Also, it's we poor people who understand it. Unfortunately, the rich don't come to hear it. Where the rich are, there's no preaching like that."

MARITA: "The rich man's sin was not sharing—not sharing with everybody, that is, with the poor, too; because he *did* share with the rich: the Gospel says he gave parties every day."

JULIO: "They weren't inviting the poor; they'd get their houses dirty."

ERNESTO: "I believe this parable was not to console the poor but rather to threaten the rich; but as you said, William, it has had the opposite effect, because the rich weren't going to heed it. But Christ himself is saying that in this parable: that the rich pay no attention to the Bible."

OSCAR: "It seems like it doesn't do any good to be reading the Bible, then, because if you don't want to change the social order, you might as well be reading any damned thing, you might as well be reading any stupid book."

ERNESTO: "It seems to me that Jesus' principal message is that the rich aren't going to be convinced even with the Bible, not even with a dead man coming to life—and not even with Jesus' resurrection."[11]

The gospel of liberation has profoundly affected the churches north of the border as well. Lenten practices in many denominations include direct action on behalf of the marginalized such as supporting shelters for battered women, advocating on behalf of the homeless, collecting supplies for local food pantries, visiting shut-ins, or participating in community organizing efforts. Congregations see themselves reversing the values of the world by heeding the voices of the last in their midst.

Transfiguration

Gazing at the mystery of the kingdom through the lens of Lent is rather like peering at a figure-ground optical illusion. In the latter, one alternately perceives two different images—typically a stemmed goblet and a pair of silhouetted faces—flip-flopping back and forth. First one image comes into focus while the other sinks back into an undifferentiated ground. Suddenly, they are reversed and one sees the second image clearly but loses sight of the first. As we plunge deeper into Lent, our present seeing is periodically confounded. What was figure becomes ground and a newly configured reality emerges clearly before our eyes. But the flip-flopping continues back and forth. We see anew. Then we see as we habitually do. Glimpses of the kingdom tease us, wary disciples that we are, into God's seeing, God's reality, God's time.

The Gospel reading for the Second Sunday of Lent is the account of the Transfiguration in one of its three forms (Matt. 17:1-9, Mark 9:2-10, Luke 9:28-36). In it, Jesus appears to several of his followers in rather the same manner as a figure-ground illusion.

> Jesus took Peter, James and John, and led them up a high mountain apart by themselves; and he was transfigured before them, and his garments became glistening, intensely white, as no one on earth could make them. And there appeared to them Elijah with Moses; and they were talking to Jesus. Peter said to Jesus, "Master, it is well that we are here; let us make three booths, one for you and one for Moses and one for Elijah." He did not know what to say; for they were exceedingly afraid. And a cloud overshadowed them, and a voice came out of the cloud, "This is my Beloved; listen to him." And suddenly looking around they no longer saw anyone with them—only Jesus.
>
> As they were coming down the mountain, Jesus charged them to tell no one what they had seen, until the Chosen one of God should have risen from the dead. They kept the matter to themselves, questioning what the rising from the dead meant.
>
> Mark 9:2-10

While it has become virtually standard in biblical commentaries to interpret the account of the transfiguration as a foresight of Jesus' resurrection, more recent exegesis has emphasized the alternative state of consciousness of the disciples who witness the event. This is very much in keeping with the spiritual reading of the passage long hallowed in the Eastern Orthodox world. The Greek fathers assumed that it was the altered perception of Peter and James and John that was the focus of the account. Their new vision allowed them a glimpse of God and the cosmos transfigured by the entire Christ event, the incarnation, crucifixion, and resurrection. Their seeing on Mount Tabor, the site assigned to the transfiguration by the Orthodox tradition, was the same panoramic seeing enjoyed by the saints in heaven. It was a sensible seeing, neither symbolic nor illusory.

The alternate state of consciousness which allows the fearful disciples to perceive Jesus anew in his glory initiates them into the hidden beauty that has been present yet, until then, unseen by them. Such alternate states of awareness were not unusual nor considered abnormal in the ancient Mediterranean world. In the same way, such states have generally been thought to be normal, if privileged, spiritual states in most religious traditions.

The disciples see into what is with new eyes. In their case, it is the teacher whose message until then they have only haltingly and dimly comprehended. Then on Mount Tabor they see sharply in the foreground what has been unavailable to them before—the magnificence of humanity transfigured by divinity, the cosmos suffused by the divine light. This is the reality of which they become visibly aware.

During our Lenten journey our habituated perceptions are likewise surprised by such a transfigured sight. This is part of the dissolution of our now, part of the creative upheaval that is often painful and disorienting in its challenge to us to change and grow into the panoramic vision offered by our God.

The Lenten time of tension between dying and birth is tinged with the hues of mystery. What we are becoming is yet unknown. The fullness of God's kingdom is visible to us only through the latticework of parable and story. We are taught that the last will be first, that our present vision of reality will be turned topsy-turvy in a celebration of the beauty hidden in the forgotten, ignored, and despised.

Seventy Times Seven

It is Lent. We enter the sanctuaries of our churches which, in not too distant memory, were brilliant with poinsettias or festooned stars, fragrant with the scent of evergreen, and poignant with choirs of preschool angels and shepherds gathered with reverent chaos around the baby in the manger. Now the sanctuary is stripped and stark. It may be draped with the penitential purple of the season. The sense of worship is reflective, even solemn. The mood is introspective. It forces us back on ourselves. We open our hymnals to the songs of the season.

Lord, who throughout these forty days
For us did fast and pray,
Teach us to overcome our sins,
And close by you to stay.

As you with Satan did contend,
And did the vict'ry win,
O give us strength in you to fight,
In you to conquer sin.

As you did hunger and did thirst,
So teach us, gracious Lord,
To die to self, and to so live
By your most holy word.

And through these days of penitence
And through your Passiontide,
For ever more in life and death,
O Lord, with us abide.

Abide with us, that through this life
Of doubts and hope and pain,
An Easter of unending joy
We may at last attain![12]

Throughout the centuries the plaintive cry, "Forgive us," has rung out in sanctuaries worldwide. In earlier eras the tone of the cry spoke primarily of our urgent need for God's forgiveness. The emphasis was upon our disheartening sinfulness, our constant turning away from the divine love extended to us. John Donne, seventeenth-century English poet, captured this repentant mood in his tripart poem, "A Hymne to God the Father." The prayer that rises from the poet's pen is deeply felt. It plumbs the hollows of a heart starkly aware of its own incapacity to grow and change to meet the demands of generous love.

I

Wilt thou forgive that sinne where I begunne,
Which is my sin, though it were done before?
Wilt thou forgive those sinnes through which I runne,
And do run still: though still I do deplore?
When thou has done, thou hast not done,
For, I have more.

II

Wilt thou forgive that sinne by which I have wonne
Others to sinne? and, made my sinne their doore?
Wilt thou forgive that sinne which I did shunne
A yeare, or two; but wallow'd in, a score?
When thou hast done, thou hast not done,
For, I have more.

III

I have a sinne of feare, that when I have spunne
My last thred, I shall perish on the shore;
But sweare by thy selfe, that at my death thy sonne
Shall shine as he shines now, and heretofore;
And, having done that, Thou hast done,
I have no more.[13]

We have modulated our communal cry for forgiveness in many of our congregations today, especially as it articulates only our own needfulness. We draw out instead the present and future reality of God's mercy which meets us unhesitatingly in the depths of our failures, stumblings, and pain. Yet forgiveness remains an insistent theme of the Lenten season: our need for divine forgiveness, our need to be forgiven by others, our need to forgive ourselves, our need to offer forgiveness to others who ask for it of us, our need to offer forgiveness to those who do not ask. The gift of forgiveness in all its faces is part of the dynamic power of this season of conversion. It is part of the heart-rending to which we are called, along with our fasting and our changing perception of what, in God's panoramic view, is to be first and what last.

Forgiving Ourselves

The cycle of Old Testament readings proclaimed throughout Lent spreads a wide and gracious mantle over the Gospel narratives that are the centerpiece of the season. The cycle situates the events of Jesus' ministry and passion in the context of salvation history. The entire sweep of the scenario is put before us: Genesis with its tales of creation and covenant, the saga of Abraham and Sarah; Exodus with its accounts of God's liberation of the Israelites, Moses and the trek toward the promised land, the revelation of the Ten Commandments; the sagas of the Judges and Kings from the historical books; and finally the fiery warnings of the prophets trumpeting out their call to the chosen people to return to their God with all their hearts.

Under this spacious canopy that tells of God's intimate dealings with humankind in history we place the Christ event, and under it we locate our own salvation histories. From this vast perspective our own brief stories are comfortingly relativized, our own failings and accomplishments are sheltered and made humble.

One of the most difficult challenges we seem to face in the spiritual journey is to love ourselves as we have been loved. There are many interpretations, both present and past, of the particularities of that challenge. I choose to focus on it from one vantage point. I call it the art of "loving our abjections." It is an art I have been exploring for a long time and one I suspect will be in need of constant practice until I die. The phrase comes from the seventeenth century Salesian spiritual tradition whose chief architects are saints Francis de Sales and Jane de Chantal.

My graduate work was focused on the lives and writings of these two saints. As I studied their writings I would frequently come across the phrase "our abjections." This at first repelled me. Whatever else I was drawn to in the language of this spiritual vision, I was certainly not drawn to what seemed a very unhealthy idea—that we should see ourselves as abject. I heard the word connoting "debased, wretched, worthless, sinners through and through." But over the years I came to another appreciation of what the idea might mean. Our "abjections" are those limiting and limited aspects of all of our lives. They are the shadowy side, the weaknesses, the brokenness that is simply a part of who we are. We can kick at it, hide it, deny it; it will not go away. In fact, the more vehemently we ignore or despise it, the more energy we have to expend to convince others and ourselves that it does not exist. Instead, we need to learn to accept our very real limitations, to allow them into our purview. But this spiritual tradition in which I was immersing myself went beyond this psychologically common sense approach. Salesian spirituality invited me to love my abjections.

I gradually came to see that I was being invited to love myself as God loved me, cognizant of the wholeness of who I am—both gifted and wounded, blessed and broken. I was being invited to forgive myself little by little for all I found unacceptable and wearisome in myself. After a time, I came to see that I was forgiving myself for simply being human. My past uncompromising self-censure suddenly seemed silly. Gradually, I came to see the profound and simultaneous blessedness and brokenness of others as well. Bit by bit, I could allow them both the fullness of their promise and the reality of their own serious limitations. Gradually, the deep ambiguity of human life was turned from a burdensome into a freeing mystery. Freed from my energetic desires to constantly "get it" and "keep it together," I could genuinely allow God to work in and through my abjections, not to make them better or neaten them up, but to allow me to be more compassionate, to judge others less, to serve them better.

Forgiving Others

If forgiving ourselves is one face of the mystery of reconciliation at the heart of the Lenten dynamic, forgiving others is another. To this adventure we are enjoined by the Gospels:

> Peter came up and said to Jesus, "Lord, how often shall my sister or my brother sin against me, and I forgive them? As many as seven times?" Jesus said to him, "I do not say to you seven times, but seventy times seven. Therefore the realm of God may be compared to a king who wished to settle accounts with his servants. When he began the reckoning, one was brought to him who owed him ten thousand talents; and as the servant could not pay, his lord ordered him to be sold, with his wife and children and all that he had, and

payment to be made. So the servant fell on his knees, imploring him, 'Lord, have patience with me, and I will pay you everything.' And out of pity for him the lord of that servant released him and forgave him the debt. But that same servant, as he went out, came upon one of his fellow servants who owed him a hundred denarii; and seizing him by the throat he said, 'Pay what you owe.' So his fellow servant fell down and besought him, 'Have patience with me, and I will pay you.' He refused and went and put him in prison till he should pay the debt. When the other servants saw what had taken place, they were greatly distressed, and they went and reported to their lord all that had taken place. Then his lord summoned him and said to him, 'You wicked servant! I forgave you all that debt because you besought me; and should not you have had mercy on your fellow servant, as I had mercy on you?' And in anger his lord delivered him to the jailers, till he should pay all his debt. So also the One who sent me will do to every one of you, if you do not forgive your sisters and brothers from your heart."

Matthew 18:21-35

The curious interplay between lord and servant, servant and servant, God and ourselves that is alluded to in this parable underscores one aspect of the mystery of forgiveness—that we are an interconnected whole, bound and unleashed by one another's capacity for generosity and graciousness. Our forgiveness of one another is not simply a matter of politeness or of grudging allowance for each other's foibles. It is instead a courageous act of defiance that refuses to remain entrapped in hatred and recrimination, and chooses instead to risk the spacious unknown of real freedom.

But genuine forgiveness is not an easily cultivated art. Especially when we have been gravely wounded by another person, our basic human dignity affronted, it is no simple task to forgive. Nor should it be done lightly. For we need also to recognize and affirm the anger, the pain, the betrayal, or the sense of injustice that we feel when genuinely hurt. Validating the injury that has occurred or acquiescing to the idea that we have rightfully been victims and deserving of our pain is not forgiveness.

Real forgiveness means balancing rightful outrage at injury with the courage to extend forgiveness to the other and unleash the bonds that hold you both enchained. But it comes slowly and, if the injury is deep, we often find ourselves coming back to the injury as the layers of our lives are peeled back and exposed in time. I think of a woman I know whose life had been cleft in two a decade earlier when her husband had reconnected with a woman he had loved in an earlier era. After much anguish, he decided to leave and return to his first love. For years this woman struggled, with the helpful aid of friends and counselors, to put her life back together, finally arriving at the point where she could let go and forgive, wishing the reunited couple well. To her dismay one Saturday she found herself seated behind her ex-husband and his now wife at the wedding of mutual acquaintances. All the old feelings she assumed she had laid aside flooded back, poisoning the air, causing her to close in on herself and withdraw her presence from the celebration. An unopened layer of her pain was laid freshly bare, calling for new courage, new generosity, new reaffirmation of her own dignity and right to be loved.

There is nothing easy about forgiveness. It draws us closely into the creative and dehabituating movement of Lent, asks us to be unmade and refashioned anew. Again and again and again, time after time after time. Yet ultimately, forgiveness is healing, both for the one who is injured and for the one who injures.

As we peer during this time of tension between dying and birth into the foreign territory of our new selves, and the new reality of the kingdom that Jesus proclaims, we get a glimpse of a reality of almost unbearable beauty.

A priest friend of mine who has worked for years as a hospital chaplain tells of his experience at a nationally known clinic for the mentally and emotionally disturbed. While many people were helped in the psychiatric holding environment of the clinic, there was a group of patients who seemed unable to make any progress in their healing. They had in common the fact that they all had been wounded deeply and found themselves unable to forgive their offenders. After years of therapy, it came down to that bare truth. A team of well-trained and qualified ministers engaged in spiritual healing were called in as a last resort. Every one of the patients was able to identify an inability to forgive as the root of his or her illness. Some could find in themselves a desire to be delivered from their inability, sensing it to be the key to their own release from suffering. Some could find available to them at least a desire to desire the gift of forgiveness. Working long and lovingly with these persons in pain, the team of healing ministers was able to bring healing into the lives of many of these formerly incurably troubled lives. Not all of them were healed, but many were. The gift of forgiveness was the key that unlocked their pain and set them free.

How astonishing: that in releasing another from being bound and identified with pain, we release ourselves as well. Well into the rhythm and texture of Lent by now in this third week, we continue to risk a free fall into the arms of a God who would remake us and make us free. We discover the deep truth of the story of the prodigal son (Luke 15:11-32)— that miraculous parable of God's loving homecoming offered for all God's children, no matter how far they have strayed, no matter how long they have been gone, no matter how deeply they are mired. There is always forgiveness. There is always welcome.

The invitation is for us to offer this to one another as well. In so doing we enter into the mystery of our intimate interconnection with one another and with God.

Loving Our Enemies

The gift of forgiveness opens the door to a new, transfigured kind of loving that, I think, is part of the changing landscape of our view during the Lenten season. It is a type of loving that is not based on natural attraction or obvious common interests or life circumstance. We may not like the other but we are called to love. We may certainly not validate or condone his or her actions. But we are called into a radical sense of our interconnectedness as creatures and children of the same God. To perceive this deep level of interdependence, especially with those whose worlds are fashioned differently than our own or perhaps with those who would seek to harm or destroy our worlds, seems a nearly impossible task. Yet the Gospels prod us on during this season of self-exploration to entertain such radical notions. At the furthest reaches of our capacities to love, we are urged, "Love even your enemies."

> But I say this to you who are listening: Love your enemies, do good to those who hate you, bless those who curse you, pray for those who treat you badly. To anyone who slaps you on one cheek, present the other cheek as well; to anyone who takes your cloak from you, do not refuse your tunic. Give to everyone who asks you, and do not ask for your property back from someone who takes it. Treat others as you would like people to treat you. If you love those who love

you, what credit can you expect? Even sinners love those who love them. And if you do good to those who do good to you, what credit can you expect? For even sinners do that much. And if you lend to those from whom you hope to get money back, what credit can you expect? Even sinners lend to sinners to get back the same amount. Instead, love your enemies and do good to them, and lend without any hope of return. You will have a great reward, and you will be children of the Most High, for he himself is kind to the ungrateful and the wicked.

Luke 6:27-36, NJB

Some echoes of the difficulty of loving one's enemy are heard in the fourth-century desert tradition. One story lets us overhear how Abba Anthony, the fabled patriarch of that tradition, challenged his disciples on this very point.

Certain of the brethren said to Abba Anthony: We would like you to tell us some word, by which we may be saved. Then the elder said: You have heard the Scriptures, they ought to be enough for you. But they said: We want to hear something also from you, Father. The elder answered them: You have heard the Lord say: If a man strikes you on the left cheek, show him also the other one. They said to him: This we cannot do. He said to them: If you can't turn the other cheek, at least take it patiently on one of them. They replied: We can't do that either. He said: If you cannot even do that, at least do not go striking others more than you would want them to strike you. They said: We cannot do this either. Then the elder said to his disciple: Go cook up some food for these brethren, for they are very weak. Finally he said to them: If you cannot even do this, how can I help you? All I can do is pray.[14]

Abba Moses is the chief character in another desert saying which underscores the idea that our forgiveness is indeed tied to the recognition of our interdependence, and our shared and fallible humanity.

A brother at Scetis committed a fault. A council was called to which Abba Moses was invited, but he refused to go to it. Then the priest sent someone to say to him, "Come, for everyone is waiting for you." So he got up and went. He took a leaking jug, filled it with water and carried it with him. The others came out to meet him and said to him, "What is this, Father?" The old man said to them, "My sins run out behind me, and I do not see them, and today I am coming to judge the errors of another." When they heard that they said no more to the brother but forgave him.[15]

Yet despite these rumblings from the early ascetic Christians, forgiveness seems to remain a theme waiting to be explored in depth in our present age. This deep and extensive kind of loving of enemies, while it has long roots in our tradition, seems to have become a theme of special urgency in the contemporary world. The annals of sanctity contain anecdotes about particular saints who have found themselves able, generally in imitation of Christ's forgiving words uttered on the cross, to express forgiveness of those who hate them. But the theme is oddly underdeveloped in the literature of the spiritual life until our times. Especially in our turbulent twentieth century, perhaps the most grim in human history in terms of sheer numbers of persons destroyed by war and famine, the hard art of forgiveness of enemies has presented itself for our consideration.

Every year in mid-February my grade-school children come home from their classrooms with mimeographed papers on which pale purple outlined portraits of the late Reverend Martin Luther King, Jr., are reproduced as a picture for them to color in. Under his visage the words, "I Have a Dream" are marked in bold print. When I ask my children about this man whose face they are filling in with a variety of Crayola shades, they are able to tell me that he was a great man who worked for black people and their rights and that he was assassinated. "What was his dream?" I ask them. They are able only to report that King wanted people to like each other and not hurt each other.

The college-aged students that I teach are not able to report a good deal more. Oh, they know something about the civil rights movement and perhaps they have seen a videotape of one of King's speeches. But what is at the root of this dream of his seems lost to our collective memory. King's entire program of militant nonviolent resistance was inspired by the principles laid out in Luke, Chapter 6, as well as other gospel narratives like Romans 12:14*ff*, where Paul instructs his correspondents to "Bless those who persecute you" and "Never repay evil with evil" and "Resist evil and conquer it with good," in which such radical forgiveness was enjoined.

King was hardly some dewy-eyed visionary who dreamed idly of people getting along. He was a committed Christian who had struggled long and hard with the gospel mandate to love one's enemy in the concrete circumstances of his own life. And what intractable and terrifying circumstances those were: the mean legacy of racial segregation and hatred long entrenched in American culture. King's dream was indeed that one day little black children and little white children might freely share the same opportunities and bounties of this nation's promise, but he was starkly realistic about the difficult road to that end. He knew that this was an undertaking of the most expansive spiritual dimension and that it would cost us dearly.

His was a vision of Lenten remaking that can challenge us as we move more deeply into the passiontide momentum of the season. Although he learned much from men like Thoreau and Gandhi along the way, the underpinnings of King's dream are sunk deep in the Gospels. He begins with the moral imperative to resist evil. Evil, in particular the evil of racial discrimination, must be resisted. It is not an option; it is an imperative. One's full humanity cannot be exercised unless this attempt is made. The question is not, "Shall I resist?" but "*How* shall I resist?" The choice is to resist evil with violent or nonviolent means. He chooses nonviolence because he sees that violent response yields only temporary solutions and merely creates more violence, while the nonviolent alternatives have the possibility of rearranging the conflict in a manner that may eventually create a genuinely new configuration.

The goal of nonviolent resistance is not victory but reconciliation, the creation of a new situation that can meet the deepest needs of both parties or sides in a conflict. To desire victory is to desire to have one's opponent crushed or defeated. This, in King's mind, could never result in his ideal, in what he called the "beloved community," in which the mutual interests that exist among even the fiercest enemies can provide the beginnings of a reconciliation that ultimately benefits all concerned.

How deeply King understood the role of forgiveness in the creation of his beloved community is seen in his assertion that the struggle for justice and the resistance against evil is not a struggle against other persons. It is rather a struggle against the structures of evil that entrap not only the oppressed but the oppressors as well. Thus the struggle against racism was not a campaign of hatred against racists but a militant resistance against racism itself which sought to release those caught on both sides of the battle from the sin of racism. "Hate the sin, love the sinner," was his motto. Revenge was to be foreign, forgiveness commonplace.

Christianity, for Dr. King, required not only that we have our own sins forgiven but that we, through forgiveness, dismantle what holds all of us in bondage. The power of forgiveness is a gift of Christ bestowed upon the community for the purpose of ushering in the kingdom, the beloved community. The power to forgive is given to us by the Holy Spirit.

In the process we must be willing to take on suffering ourselves rather than inflict harm on others. We must renounce not only the use of physical violence but the internal spirit of violence as well. We must genuinely love our enemies, not sentimentally, not because we like them or find their actions comprehensible, but because we have been challenged to do so by the Gospels. In this we find cosmic accompaniment, which, King believed, was aligned ultimately with the emergence of justice.

Forgiveness stands at the heart of the Lenten experience: forgiveness of ourselves, forgiveness of others, forgiveness of our enemies. In dying, our God was revealed to be one who forgave even those responsible for that death. What greater intimacy, what greater experience of loving God could we seek than to be persons who also forgive?

Refreshment

During Lent of 1994, the week after burying my father, I went on retreat. My husband, children, and I had flown back from my home town in California to Nebraska where we live, and I took several days to drive into the rural countryside. The winter had been cold, not excessively snowy, but raw and tiring, as only prairie winters can be. Now the weather was teasing us with touches of pre-springtime temperatures. The prairie was still painted in shades of brown and straw with accents of white where snow patches yet unmelted nested in sunless ravines. The icy blue of the sky stretched unbroken except for the periodic stark grey outlines of leafless trees planted in stern rows to shoulder the brunt of the arctic winds that threaten to make life uninhabitable here. No hint of green as yet was to be seen. But the raw cold had lifted and the hope of spring was in the air.

On the drive out to my destination, I stopped to hunt out the legendary sandhill cranes that travel north-south and back again across the migratory throughway that cuts down central Nebraska. Early March through late April is the season that they stop on their way northward to feed and gather strength for the upcoming breeding season. It was somewhat early for their arrival, but I was informed that I might be able to view at least a few of the graceful birds that attract the attention of scores of appreciative viewers yearly and have inspired heartland poets and naturalists with their exquisite inflight beauty and fascinating landed behavior. With the help of local maps and the eager directions of locals in roadside cafes, I made my way off the interstate to the dirt side roads along the Platte River where sandhill cranes might be seen en route to their breeding grounds.

I located several flocks that were feeding in the fields on the west side of the highway and stopped for awhile to watch from the blind of my car. I had been instructed to stay inside lest I frighten off the notoriously nervous birds; besides it was still too cold to enjoy being outside. The brochure from the nearest town's Chamber of Commerce informed me that the daily habits of the crane included settling for the night on the sandbars and shallows of the Platte, a lifting off at sunrise (spectacular at the height of the season when the cranes' population is high), and landing in the fields where the cranes "loaf and dance" for the remainder of the day until sundown when there is another liftoff and return to the river. It was midafternoon when I located my flock, so I settled down to observe the loafing and dancing of the cranes.

They were wonderful. Long-necked, sinewy creatures arcing splendidly across the sky in triads or swirling up by the score out of the resting flock and settling back down between the stubbled rows of corn or soy stalks to face one another in a *pas de deux* of wing lifting and leg prancing. I was enchanted by them and gave myself over to the spirit of loafing and dancing that I was watching. Despite the low temperatures, the Lenten season, and the fresh memories of my father's burial, the birds' presence somehow spoke of a secret hidden in the colorless late winter landscape.

Two days later, as I traveled the same road eastward home, the temperatures had risen. The sky, empty on my ride west, was now strewn from horizon to horizon with necklaces of migrating birds, ducks, and geese. As far as the eye could see there were phalanxes, swarms, arrows, and queues of flying creatures, falling like handfuls of tossed confetti or launching themselves with powerful, thrusting strokes in purposeful parades. The birds filled the sky. I opened my car windows, shut since the fall, and let their honking, singing, and wing-beating enter my wintery world with the first warm breezes of virgin spring.

The birds were harbingers of the new life that emerges from death, the gentle freshness of spring to which harsh winter finally yields. In the midst of that Lent with its somber colors and its sadness of loss, a few days were given me to dance and loaf with the sandhill cranes.

A Moment of Refreshment

The Lenten season too has its harbinger of spring, its brief taste of Easter during the fourth week. This day, known as Laetare or Rejoice Sunday (named for the first word of the traditional introit from Isaiah "Rejoice, O Jerusalem"), is celebrated with rose-colored vestments and a slight lightening of the solemn Lenten mood. The Church of England customarily refers to the day as Refreshment Sunday or Mothering Sunday. Customs of visiting one's mother or baking and eating similcakes are still occasionally practiced today.

Many of the readings for Laetare Sunday capture the anticipatory mood by playing with the theme of light emerging from darkness. Mirroring the natural processes of the earth that is emerging from winter's limited daylight into the longer sunlit days of spring, the liturgical celebration plays with the light and darkness theme in a variety of ways. Passages from Ephesians (5:8-14) which enjoin those now in the light of Christ to walk as children of light and not of darkness especially underscore this theme. In one of the readings from the Gospel of John, Nicodemus, a respected elder in the Jewish community, comes to Jesus under cover of night (lest he be seen with the suspicious rabbi) to engage him in religious conversation. They speak together of the spiritual mystery of being born again, of eternal life, and of God's sending a son into the world. The conversation ends with an assertion that the light has come into the world but that some have loved darkness rather than light.

The light in darkness theme, clearly anticipatory of the coming Easter motif of dawning light that we will enact so dramatically at the Easter vigil, is also present in the Johannine story of the man born blind, proclaimed during this fourth Lenten week (John 9:1-41). In this parable, we learn of a man blind from birth who was presumed to be so because of his or his parents' sin. Referring to himself as the light of the world, Jesus singles him out for healing. Making clay out of the ground on which he spits, Jesus bestows sight on the man. This causes consternation among some of the religious leaders who end up casting the man out, despite his witness to Jesus' extraordinary, divinely given powers of healing. The motif of the light of God piercing the darkness of the blind man's world yet remaining unseen by the dark spirits of those unable to perceive the dawning light animates the reading. The light image comes to us as refreshment and welcome respite during this somber season.

Scattered throughout the Lenten season are also scripture readings that enliven us with their evocation of waters that nourish and refresh. Our thirsty hearts, parched from our sojourn in the desert, are met with the springtime promise of the prophet Hosea in a passage charged with overtones of the coming Eastertide.

> In their distress they seek me, saying:
> "Come, let us return to our God;
> for you, O God, have torn, that you may heal us;
> you have stricken, and you will bind us up.

After two days you will revive us;
  on the third day you will raise us up,
that we may live before you.

Let us know, let us press on to know you, O God;
  your going forth is sure as the dawn;
you will come to us as the showers,
  as the spring rains that water the earth."

Hosea 6:1-3

The same theme of watering, this time with river waters that nurture new life and effect healing, is reiterated by the prophet Ezekiel in an extraordinary prophetic vision that speaks of waters issuing from the threshold of the Jerusalem temple.

Then I was led back along the bank of the river. As I went back, I saw upon the bank of the river very many trees on the one side and on the other. The messenger of God said to me, "This water flows toward the eastern region and goes down into the Arabah; and when it enters the stagnant waters of the sea, the water will become fresh. Wherever the river goes every living creature which swarms will live, and there will be very many fish; for this water goes there, that the waters of the sea may become fresh; so everything will live where the river goes. And on the banks, on both sides of the river, there will grow all kinds of trees for food. Their leaves will not wither nor their fruit fail, but they will bear fresh fruit every month, because the water for them flows from the sanctuary. Their fruit will be for food, and their leaves for healing."

Ezekiel 47:7-12

God comes as the rain and as the river currents to refresh and revitalize the lifeless soil of our lives. God comes from without, as gift and grace. God also comes from within, as the bottomless spring that sustains the roots of our beings. The prophet Jeremiah proclaims this truth with an unforgettable image of trees planted by water.

Blessed are they who trust in God,
  whose trust is the Most High.
They are like a tree planted by water,
  that sends out its roots by the stream,
and does not fear when heat comes,

> for its leaves remain green,
> and is not anxious in the year of drought,
> for it does not cease to bear fruit.

Jeremiah 17:7-8

So too the theme of sustaining water is heard in the Johannine Gospel account known as the Woman at the Well. The passage begins as Jesus comes to a city in Samaria named Sychar near a spot known as Jacob's Well. There he encounters a Samaritan woman come to draw water.

> A woman of Samaria came to draw water. Jesus said to her, "Give me a drink." His followers had gone away into the city to buy food. The Samaritan woman said to him, "How is it that you, a Jew, ask a drink of me, a woman of Samaria?" For Jews have no dealings with Samaritans. Jesus answered her, "If you knew the gift of God, and who it is that is saying to you, 'Give me a drink,' you would have asked him, and he would have given you living water." The woman said to him, "Sir, you have nothing to draw with, and the well is deep; where do you get that living water? Are you greater than our ancestors Rachel and Jacob, who gave us the well, and drank from it themselves, and their children, and their cattle?" Jesus said to her, "Every one who drinks of this water will thirst again, but whoever drinks of the water that I shall give, will never thirst; the water that I shall give will become in that person a spring of water welling up to eternal life." The woman said to him, "Sir, give me this water, that I may not thirst, nor come here to draw."

John 4:7-15

Water that gushes forth in abundance, sustaining and generating life, this is what is promised. So too, in this dry desert season of the heart, we are watered by God's promise of sustenance and fullness of life to come.

Divine Mothering

I find this mid-Lenten gentling of mood delightfully feminine and comfortingly maternal. It speaks to me of a divine inclination sung in the words of the familiar hymn:

> *There's a wideness in God's mercy*
> *Like the wideness of the sea.*
> *There's a kindness in God's justice*
> *Which is more than liberty.*[16]

Our Lenten remaking is not limited to the taut discernment of the wilderness, the disorienting reversals of values, or the free fall into radical forgiveness. We are reminded in this fourth week that our first hesitating steps toward the kingdom proclaimed are taken at God's own knee. With a mother's solicitude, God's wide mercy and kindly justice support and steady us. From babes-in-arms to lap-sitters to porch-crawlers to yard-players, we remain within the encircling presence of God's tender, watchful care as we mature through the seasons of our lives.

God mothers us through the season-in-between in many ways. Most foundationally, God is the hidden ground out of which we came and have being. As I grope around the far recesses of my own memories for analogies to this hidden divine mothering, two women emerge. Both were for me the inarticulate and primal ground of love from which I came forth. First, there is my actual mother.

Several years ago, as I was reflecting on my faith journey, I became aware that my mother held a very unusual place in my remembered life. Childhood memories, of which I have many, have always been filled with a vivid sense of place—the sturdy walnut treehouse in which I spent imaginative hours, the downstairs bedroom with walk-in closets in which I constructed a mansion for my dolls, the living room corner of my grandfather's house where I played with glass figurines from his what-not while awaiting Thanksgiving dinner. I have strong memories of people who filled those places as well: the sweet, dry, powdered smell of my father's mother as she sat on the couch in our house at Christmastime, the pungent scent of fingernail lacquer applied by my older cousin as we crouched on the sunny steps of my uncle's suburban ranch-style house on Fourth of July. But as I looked back over my life, I discovered that I had few vivid sensory memories of my mother. I could only call her forth as background, as the one who provided the foundation out of which my world emerged. I could recall her offices located in the different homes we inhabited, always furnished with the same well-used typewriter. I could reconstruct the bedrooms she shared with my father, the kitchens she bustled about in, the sewing rooms hung with fabric for Halloween costumes. But with rare exceptions, I could not call her up in memory as I could other people. Not that I experienced her as absent. Quite the opposite. She was extraordinarily present. It was as though in memory she were standing behind me rather than in front of me, present to provide any encouragement, support, or protection I might require but not in the foreground of attention. At first this troubled me. Then I began to see what a gift she was. She had become the hidden ground of love that provided the backdrop for all the loving that I was to do in my life—love of place and love of people. And I began to accept her mothering presence in this way.

So too God is the hidden ground of love, the matrix out of which we emerge and go about the business of our lives. Constantly present yet only occasionally in the forefront of consciousness, this unnoticed divine mothering sustains and supports us.

The second woman I think of is an even more hidden figure in my childhood past. Her name was Josephine. She was an older black woman hired by my parents after my birth to come and assist my mother with the work of childrearing. Josephine was with us full time for at least two years and part time for another two. Until I was in my forties my only recollection of Josephine was of a photo in a family album of me, about six, standing uncomfortably next to a tall, thin, elderly black woman dressed in a housecoat and sandals on the sidewalk outside our Los Angeles house. Presumably, Josephine had paid a visit to the little girl she had so patiently raised several years earlier, and the little girl had awkwardly agreed to pose with this woman who was now for her a stranger. I had too a memory of the few stories my mother had shared about Josephine: that she had raised a large family herself, that her parents were slaves, that she was illiterate, that she carried with her that self-effacing diffidence born of her history, that she refused to eat with my parents at the lunch table at their house, that she had loved me like her own child, that she had fed and changed and potty-trained me and taught me to walk and to talk with the easy good humor and delight born of long familiarity with small children, that I had adored Josephine, and that when my parents felt her services were no longer needed, she had gone away.

Years later, when early childhood literature began to stress the importance of infant-adult bonding, my mother expressed to me some concern that the abrupt departure from my life of someone as central as Josephine must have been traumatic for me. But I had no recollection of any trauma nor of Josephine herself. It never dawned on me to pursue the issue.

Decades later, I was acting as faculty member at a program for spiritual formation held by The United Methodist Church. My faculty colleague was a woman engaged in the study of religion and depth psychology. Her presentations involved, among other things, engaging students in meditation techniques to heal past painful memories. I decided to join the students and experience the processes she taught. About halfway through the session she introduced a meditation to heal forgotten memories. Odd, I thought, but worth trying. I lay down on the carpet as we were instructed and began to listen to her guided reflections. "Return to your childhood home," she began. Suddenly I found myself flashing back through a series of dwellings in which my parents and I had lived. I lost track of the facilitator's voice and found myself in the living room of the house where I had been born. The next thing I knew I was in a tunnel of bright light walking toward an approaching figure that I could not make out because of the brilliancy of the light. As the figure came nearer, I began to have some sense of its identity. It was Josephine, looking very much the same as she had in the photo in the family album, only she was wearing a full length apron over her cotton housedress. I knew at once that I had never had an opportunity to say goodbye to her and that this weighed on my heart at a level at which I was consciously unaware. Josephine and I moved toward one another in the bright tunnel. When we met she addressed me in a diffident tone, "Well, well, well, what a fine woman you have become. How many things you have done! What a smart woman! And how many things you *know*." She nodded her head at me. Something welled up in me in protest. The knowing that I had arrived at, I knew, could not be attributed to my degrees, my writing, my education. I found myself exclaiming, "No, Josephine. Don't you realize that everything I know about God first came from you?"

We embraced in the blazing tunnel and she retreated. The grief of our unacknowledged relationship and our abrupt parting hit me and I wept. How strange it all seemed. The memory of a woman of whom I had no conscious recollection lay deep in my heart, in the marrow of my bone, it felt like. Somewhere imprinted on my flesh was the feel of her caress, the knowledge of her lifting embrace, the sight of her encouraging smiles. She was God-bearer for me. What was her faith? How had she communicated it to me nonverbally in my early years? I do not know the answer to any of those questions, but they speak profoundly to my sense of God as mothering presence.

Josephine was for me the hidden mothering, the selfless, loving attention of God so remote from my conscious activity that it is unremembered. Yet I have been tended, loved, and supported by divine love all along, from before the time of memory's arising.

God's maternal solicitude is for us love's hidden ground. But God also mothers us in other ways. The spiritual tradition to which we are heir contains many allusions to God's mothering. It is especially in the mystical tradition that the motherhood of God is given expression: God as the one whose body feeds us; God as the one who labors and gives us new life on the cross; God whose creative activity confers life on us. These themes unfold for us beyond Lent in the dynamics of Holy Week, when in the Maundy Thursday liturgy we come to experience ourselves as a communion of shared hunger, fed by God and feeding one another; on Good Friday when our new life is born of the agony, the blood, and the water of the cross; and at the Easter Vigil when God's cosmic fecundity is proclaimed in the imagery of the creation narratives of Genesis.

Now, on this Mothering Sunday we are refreshed by glimpses of God's hidden nurture. And we rejoice. We pray the introit for the day which continues with a rapturous passage that captures all of the varied motifs of this mid-Lent Sunday: refreshment and mothering; nurturing in the form of watering and of being suckled.

> Rejoice with Jerusalem,
> be glad for her, all you who love her!
> Rejoice, rejoice with her,
> all you who mourned her!
>
> So that you may be suckled and satisfied
> from her consoling breast,
> so that you may drink deep with delight
> from her generous nipple.
>
> For Yahweh says this:
> Look, I am going to send peace
> flowing over her like a river,
> and like a stream in spate
> the glory of the nations.

You will be suckled, carried on her hip
and fondled in her lap.
As a mother comforts a child,
so I shall comfort you;
you will be comforted in Jerusalem.

Isaiah 66:10-13, NJB

Like children pressed to the breast or cradled in arms, we come to know the tender presence of our God.

To Touch the Wounds

The last two weeks of Lent, in earlier years known as Passiontide, are characterized by a growing sense of darkness and inevitability. The momentum of the season draws us inexorably into the mystery of the crucifixion on our way to the Resurrection. The passageway is a narrow one. Much like a pregnant woman's realization, as she comes close to term, that there is only one possible route to take to finally hold her child in her arms, through the intense and unknown drama of labor and birth, we are compelled by the gathering energy of the coming passion.

For centuries the passion of Christ has been enacted as religious theater through the devotional practice of the Stations of the Cross. Entering into Jesus' final suffering by praying—visually, verbally, and bodily—with the fourteen pictures or carvings depicting Jesus' last journey from his trial to his entombment is a familiar Lenten devotion for many Christians.

The standard presentation of the Stations today takes place in the nave of the church, generally on each Friday of Lent. Hung around the walls are the fourteen images of Jesus' journey produced by the collective imagination of Christendom: Jesus is condemned by Pilate; he takes up his cross; he falls the first time; he meets his mother; Simon of Cyrene is made to bear the cross; Veronica wipes his face; he falls the second time; he meets the women of Jerusalem; he falls a third time; he is stripped of his garments; he is nailed to the cross; he dies; his body is taken down from the cross; he is laid in the tomb. Led by a presider, typically the participants in the Stations move from one image to the next where a meditation on the particular moment depicted is read and a prayer recited. Often the procession in between each Station is accompanied by music, especially the ancient hymn Stabat Mater, whose text was composed in the thirteenth century by the Franciscan spiritual writer, Jacapone da Todi.

> At the cross her station keeping,
> Mary stood in sorrow, weeping,
> When her Son was crucified.

While she waited in her anguish,
Seeing Christ in torment languish,
Bitter sorrow pierced her heart.

With what pain and desolation,
With what noble resignation,
Mary watched her dying Son.

Ever patient in her yearning,
Though her tear-filled eyes were burning,
Mary gazed upon her Son.[17]

The practice of the Stations presumably grew out of the desire of medieval pilgrims to reproduce at home the pilgrim route from Pilate's house to Calvary that they had followed in Jerusalem. At a more primary level, the devotion expresses the religious aesthetic of late medieval Christianity which perdures in some circles until today, an aesthetic which would focus on the suffering of Jesus as the central and most clearly redemptive dynamic of the Christ event.

For centuries, Christians in the western church, in myriad ways, have lingered at the foot of the cross wonderingly and have been drawn to that cross-hung figure, so much so that they wished to enter into the actual experience itself. Meditation books and exercises on the Passion are a standard feature of medieval and early modern Catholic spirituality. Mystics and monastics have left us ample literary evidence of their devotion to the Passion and their intimate participation in that drama by affectively identifying with the pain and sorrow of Christ's march to Calvary. Through love these Christ-followers entered into the dying that would finally issue in new life. One such example from the fourteenth century is Margaret Ebner, a German nun of the Dominican Order. In her *Revelations*, Margaret recalls her own experience of living the Passion. Her account begins as she was at communal morning prayer (matins).

> When I began matins the greatest pain came over my heart and also a sorrow, so bitter that it was as if I were really in the presence of my Beloved, my most heartily Beloved One, and as if I had seen His most painful sufferings with my own eyes and as if all were happening before me at that very moment. Until that time I had never yet perceived true suffering in my whole life. My pain and the

bitterness of my sorrow were so great that I thought nothing more painful could ever have happened to another human being, and I do not wish to exclude St. Mary Magdalen. When I had read three lessons of matins I could not read anymore. This present suffering lasted until matins had been sung. They laid me down and it was so painful for me that I would have given myself up to death: indeed nothing in the world seemed more desirable and delightful to me than to die in the love and in the pain of my Lord's sufferings. I lay in bed in the dormitory—not in the room near the choir—since I could not bear to hear the singing. I was sick until after prime. I could neither read matins nor the other hours of the day. Indeed I could not utter a word due to my sickness. I could only make a sign that I wanted to receive the Holy Body of our Lord. Thereupon our confessor came to me. . . .

During the night of the Vigil I heard someone swearing by the holy suffering of my Lord. That happened to me again in the same way and lasted throughout the year. But when I was given to loud exclamations and Outcries by the gentle goodness of God (these were given to me when I heard the holy sufferings spoken about), then I was pierced to the heart and this extended to all my members, and I was then bound and evermore strongly grasped by the Silence. In these cases I sit a long time—sometimes longer, sometimes shorter. After this my heart was as if shot by a mysterious force. Its effect rose up to my head and passed on to all my members and broke them violently. Compelled by the same force I cried out loudly and exclaimed. I had no power over myself and was not able to stop the Outcry until God released me from it. Sometimes it grasped me so powerfully that red blood spurted from me. Then such sorrow came over me that I thought I could not endure life for long. It would be a great consolation for me to die of this love. My Lord Jesus Christ showed His ever present help to me: at its passing it left me truly happy in sweet grace and I remained so for two days.[18]

Such baroque expressions of identification with Christ may be very foreign to our twentieth-century sensibilities. They may also be antithetical to the sensibilities of some denominations that have so stressed the idea of Jesus' substitution for us that any affective proximity to the crucifixion is perceived as a denial of God's saving grace. Nevertheless, such sentiments are anything but unusual in the tradition. Christians have from the beginning entered into the Christ event in quite dramatic and emotive ways. They have desired to be somehow *inside* the process of dying so that they might be brought to new life with Christ. This compelling idea continues to express itself in a variety of ways in our contemporary context. For example, it is evidenced when the Stations of the Cross are adapted to the justice concerns of modern Christianity. Instead of focusing on the historical passion of Christ or on the personal, mystical sharing in the Passion, the Passion is seen to take place in the pain and rejection of the poor and marginalized of our society. The prayer of the Stations becomes a prayer of God's and our solidarity with those who suffer.

It has become tradition for the Christian community in Omaha, Nebraska, where I live, to sponsor such a reenactment of the Stations of the Cross at noon on Good Friday each year. A large crowd gathers in downtown Omaha at a church centrally located near several area shelters and soup kitchens. The service takes nearly two hours as participants process from the church to the shelter for battered women, to the Dorothy Day House of Hospitality, to the Francis House which provides nighttime shelter for the homeless, and so forth. The somewhat motley crowd is led by a celebrant carrying a life-sized wooden cross. The worshipers wind their way through the city streets singing: "Were you there when they crucified my Lord?" The meditations read at the various stations identify the ancient suffering of Christ with the present day suffering of the marginalized in our society.

Touch that Heals

Even as we are drawn inexorably into the momentum of Passiontide, we are liturgically teased into remembering the majestic and glorious side of the upcoming events we celebrate. Among the readings for the Fifth Sunday of Lent is John's account of the raising of Lazarus. The story tells of one Lazarus of Bethany who, with his sisters, Mary and Martha, is a friend of Jesus. Lazarus falls ill and the sisters send for their friend to effect a cure. Jesus, however, does not arrive in time, and Lazarus dies. According to John, Jesus is aware of the death and seems to advise his followers that it will be the occasion of their belief in him. The miracle arouses the ire of the religious authorities and sets in motion the chain of events that will eventually result in Jesus' arrest.

When Jesus came, he found that Lazarus had already been in the tomb four days. Bethany was near Jerusalem, about two miles off, and many had come to Martha and Mary to console them concerning their brother. When Martha heard that Jesus was coming, she went and met him, while Mary sat in the house. Martha said to Jesus, "Lord, if you had been here, my brother would not have died. Even now I know that whatever you ask from God, God will give you." Jesus said to her, "Your brother will rise again." Martha said to him, "I know that he will rise again in the resurrection at the last day." Jesus said to her, "I am the resurrection and the life; those who believe in me, though they die, yet shall they live, and whoever lives and believes in me shall never die. Do you believe this?" She said to him, "Yes, Lord; I believe that you are the Christ, the Son of God, who is coming into the world."

When she had said this, she went and called her sister Mary, saying quietly, "The Teacher is here and is calling for you." When Mary heard it, she rose quickly and went to him. Now Jesus had not yet come to the village, but was still in the place where Martha had met him. When those who were with her in the house, consoling her, saw Mary rise quickly and go out, they followed her, supposing that she was going to the tomb to weep there. Then Mary, when she came where Jesus was and saw him, fell at his feet, saying to him, "Lord, if you had been here, my brother would not have died." When Jesus saw her weeping, and those who came with her also weeping, he was deeply moved in spirit and troubled; and he said, "Where have you laid him?" They said to him, "Lord, come and see." Jesus wept. So they said, "See how he loved him!" But some of them said, "Could not he who opened the eyes of the blind man have kept this man from dying?"

Then Jesus, deeply moved again, came to the tomb; it was a cave, and a stone lay upon it. Jesus said, "Take away the stone." Martha, the sister of the dead man, said to him, "Lord, by this time there will be an odor, for he has been dead four days." Jesus said to her, "Did I not tell you that if you would believe you would see the glory of God?" So they took away the stone. Jesus lifted up his eyes and said, "O God, I thank you that you have heard me. I know that you hear me always, but I have said this on account of the people standing by, that they may believe that you did send me." When he had said this, he cried with a loud voice, "Lazarus, come out." The dead man came out, his hands and feet bound with bandages, and his face wrapped with a cloth. Jesus said to them, "Unbind him, and

let him go." Many who had come with Mary and had seen what he
did, believed in him.

John 11:17-45

The account of the raising of Lazarus is a wonder marveled at by
generations of Christians. It speaks of God's redemptive action in the
midst of human life, of divine fulfillment of the ancient covenant in the
person of Jesus. It proclaims Jesus as the Christ, the fount of eternal life.

Beyond this, the Johannine passage is an incredibly rich mine of
images and ideas that can enliven its hearers. It contains the poignant
account of Jesus' friendship with this family, the encounter with the
weeping Mary with her distraught accusation—"If you had been here"—
and the episode of Jesus' tearful response to her grief. Even more strikingly,
it contains Martha's confession that Jesus is the Messiah, the Son of God.
Except for the confession of Peter found in Matthew 16:16 (and the
confession of Andrew to Peter in John 1:41), there is no other comparable
statement of faith discovered in the gospels. For the early church, to
confess Christ in this way was the mark of an apostle. Thus we have here a
somewhat lost tradition, apparently current in the community from which
the Gospel of John comes, of Martha as a first witness to Jesus as the
resurrection, the one who brings new life.

The Lazarus passage, placed here strategically in the heart of
Passiontide, speaks eloquently to me of hope and healing, especially as it is
discovered in the communities of friendship in which we find ourselves. It
is a Gospel that speaks of tears and compassion and the empathetic
suffering we share with one another, a suffering which raises us beyond
our own small sorrows and limited vision. It is a Gospel that proclaims the
miracle of renewal that is discovered as we allow ourselves to know our
interdependence. Our personal lifelessness, our private wounds are made
whole as we tenderly touch and are touched by one another.

So many of the healing narratives in the New Testament carry that
message. Jesus touches and is touched by scores of broken, sorrowing
people. He rubs spittle on the eyes of a blind man (Mark 8:22-26), a
hemorrhaging woman reaches out to grasp his cloak (Mark 5:25-34), he
cures Peter's mother-in-law of fever by touching her hand (Matt. 8:14-15;
Mark 1:29-31); he raises Jairus's daughter to life by taking her hand (Mark
5:21-43), and a woman bent double for eighteen years is able to stand

straight as he lays his hands on her (Luke 13:10-13). Jesus is also recorded as healing simply through speech, calling Lazarus forth from the tomb, commanding spirits to leave those possessed, and telling the paralyzed to walk. But all of the healing narratives point to the same mysterious power of healing that takes place between people. The stories of touch are simply more dramatic and concrete examples of that fundamental truth.

This truth of the power of our interconnectedness was brought home to me in an unexpected way not long ago. One recent spring I was referred by my family physician to an endocrinologist because of a growth on the right lobe of my thyroid, which had become visible at the front of my neck. After blood tests and a series of radioactive iodine scans, the specialist informed me that he needed to perform a biopsy on the growth to gain the necessary information he needed to make an accurate diagnosis. This procedure involved placing several small needles into the lump in my neck and drawing out tissue which would then be analyzed at the laboratory. It was not a terrifically painful procedure, he assured me, but there would be pain and discomfort involved. While he could freeze the surface skin where the needles would enter, anesthetizing anything beneath the surface would not be possible. Perhaps the worst part of the biopsy would be having to submit to the inserting of the sharp needles into that most vulnerable part of my person.

Vulnerable *was* what I felt when the biopsy began. To get clear access to the growth, I was asked to lie on the examination table and prop a pillow under my shoulder blades and upper back so that my head fell backwards off the pillow and left my throat prominently exposed. Trying to keep the mood light while he unwrapped the long sharp implements from their sterile casings, the endrocronologist (who had learned earlier that I taught in a theology department) made a clever comment about the story of Abraham and his son, Isaac. I *did* feel like Isaac docilely submitting to the one in whom I had placed trust.

Because my head was tilted back I could mainly see the office walls and, if I looked hard out of the side of my eye, the physician towering above my shoulder and neck. My hands were clasped across my middle and I remember wondering if they would ask me to make a fist the way one does when one gives blood. Just before the physician inserted the first needle, one of the two nurse assistants who were standing by his side toward the end of the exam table took my hands in hers. I could not see which nurse it was but I knew immediately what she expected me to do—hold on to her. That is in fact what I did. As each of the needles was inserted deep into my throat, I found myself communicating my response to the pain to her hands. As the pain rose I held tighter, as it subsided I let go. I remember thinking that she had remarkable hands, healer's hands, that they "said" much more than simply, "Hang on here if you have to."

Deep empathy flowed through her hands as she watched the procedure and felt it with me. And in a strange way, the consciousness of my pain flowed out away from me into my hands and beyond them into hers. When the doctor asked midway, "How is this feeling?" I responded, "The hands help." I never did learn which of the nurses held my hands because when they helped me upright after the biopsy was finished, the two of them were busy preparing the smears on the slides for the lab.

I did not think very deeply about the experience (except to reflect on the fact that I felt a bit shaky walking out of the office and to run through the list of possible outcomes from the biopsy the endocrinologist had enumerated) until later that day. About four o'clock, driving to pick up my children after school, suddenly the experience came rushing back to me. In the recalling, parts of the experience that I had not been aware of now became vividly clear. First, the utter vulnerability of the position hit me: the throat with its tender, life-sustaining arteries exposed. Second, I became aware of the inner shift that had occurred when I took the unknown nurse's hands. I had been making the kind of inner preparation that I might usually make, a sort of burrowing down into myself to find the resource, strength, or attitude that could get me through, when suddenly I found myself connected to a source of strength outside myself, a self-transcending energy that was greater than my bounded efforts and capacities. It was a graced moment, a grateful recognition of the holy, if you will, and, flooded with gratitude for it, I broke into tears.

This late Lenten Sunday is one in which we enter into the mystery of pain and brokenness, both our own and the world's, to discover that we are not alone, that what seems hopeless is in fact hope-filled, that what appears dead can spring forth in life. It happens because we are embedded in a wider, more sustaining matrix of love than we can possibly imagine.

HOLY WEEK

And can it be that I should gain
    An interest in the Savior's blood?
Died he for me, who caused his pain?
    For me? Who him to death pursued?
Amazing love! How can it be
That thou, my God, shouldst die for me?

'Tis myst'ry all: th' Immortal dies!
    Who can explore his strange design?
In vain the firstborn seraph tries
    To sound the depths of love divine.
'Tis mercy all! Let earth adore!
Let angel minds inquire no more.

He left his Father's throne above
    (So free, so infinite his grace!),
Emptied himself of all but love,
    And bled for Adam's helpless race.
'Tis mercy all, immense and free,
    For, O my God, it found out me!

Long my imprisoned spirit lay,
    Fast bound in sin and nature's night.
Thine eye diffused a quick'ning ray;
    I woke; the dungeon flamed with light.
My chains fell off, my heart was free,
I rose, went forth, and followed thee.

No condemnation now I dread,
    Jesus, and all in him, is mine.
    Alive in him, my living head,
    And clothed in righteousness divine,
Bold I approach th' eternal throne,
And claim the crown, through Christ my own.

CHARLES WESLEY
Hymn 193, 1780
Hymnbook[19]

Behold Your King!

When they drew near to Jerusalem and came to Bethphage, to the Mount of Olives, Jesus sent two of his companions, saying to them, "Go into the village opposite you, and immediately you will find an ass tied, and a colt with her; untie them and bring them to me. If any one says anything to you, you shall say, 'The Lord has need of them,' and he will send them immediately." This took place to fulfill what was spoken by the prophet, saying,

"Tell the daughter of Zion,
Behold, your king is coming to you,
humble, and mounted on an ass,
and on a colt, the foal of an ass."

They went and did as Jesus had directed them; they brought the ass and the colt, and put their garments on them, and he sat thereon. Most of the crowd spread their garments on the road, and others cut branches from the trees and spread them on the road. And the crowds that went before him and that followed him shouted, "Hosanna to the Son of David! Blessed is the one who comes in the name of our God! Hosanna in the highest!" When he entered Jerusalem, all the city was stirred, saying, "Who is this?" And the crowds said, "This is the prophet Jesus from Nazareth of Galilee."

Matthew 21:1-11

We gather in the narthex of the church or on the steps outside if the chill of virgin spring has worn off enough to allow it. We are packed close together, small children huddled next to their parents in the unfamiliar crush. We clutch the palm branches we have been handed and imagine ourselves, two thousand years ago, in a similar crowd on a road outside Jerusalem. We anticipate with great excitement the arrival of the infamous prophet from Nazareth. Rumor has it he has come to set us free.

All glory, laud and honor
To you, Redeemer King
To whom the lips of children
Made sweet hosannas ring.

(The organist opens all the stops and the triumphal chords
buoy up our full-throated singing.)

You are the King of Israel,
And David's royal Son,
Now in the Lord's Name coming,
Our King and Blessed one.[21]

We crowd around the celebrant/King and press forward into the
holy city/church, waving our palms, celebrating the triumphal arrival with
hosannas of joy.

Crowded together at the Jerusalem gates, we expect a political
leader, a warrior-king of the line of David come to free Israel from the
yoke of Roman domination. The palms we wave are a political statement,
for the palm has been the symbol of Israel's sovereignty since the time of
the Maccabean revolt.

But we do not get the leader we have anticipated. For instead of
entering the holy city on a warhorse, this Jesus comes deliberately on an
ass's colt, thereby calling up our collective memory of the prophecy in
Zechariah which paints for us a picture of a monarch who bans
implements of war, whose rule is gentle and whose reign is peace.

Rejoice heart and soul, daughter of Zion,
Shout for joy, daughter of Jerusalem!
Look, your king is approaching,
he is vindicated and victorious,
humble and riding on a donkey,
on a colt, the foal of a donkey.
He will banish chariots from Ephraim
and horses from Jerusalem;
the bow of war will be banished.
He will proclaim peace to the nations,
his empire will stretch from sea to sea,
from the River to the limits of the earth.
Zechariah 9:9-10, NJB

The antihero rides into Jerusalem on the back of a donkey. The
Gospel writers (the entry into Jerusalem is found in all four Gospels in
variant forms) of course could see in hindsight that Jesus' reign would be

instituted in a totally unexpected way, through his ignominious death. That he is a king of uncommon means is clear in all the Gospel accounts, but John heightens this perception by placing the anointing of Jesus by Mary of Bethany directly before his entry into Jerusalem. The Johannine account links this gesture of anointing, reserved often for kings, with Jesus' prophetic statement, "You will not always have me with you." Anointing here is both for burial and to designate royalty. Jesus' ultimate victory is to be accomplished by means we in the expectant throngs could never have imagined.

We have entered into Holy Week, the moment of greatest depth, wonder, and solemnity in the Christian liturgical year. The mood is theatrical. The air is electric with excitement.

The Suffering Servant

The rites we associate with Palm Sunday are ancient ones dating back to the fourth century. The Christian community in all its denominational expressions celebrates this Sunday before Easter in much the same way, reenacting Jesus' festal entry into Jerusalem. But denominations differ on the ways they reenact the rest of the week. All retell the same story, yet some tend to sustain the mood of this festal scene in anticipation of the great feast of Easter while others pause in the festive mood only briefly before plunging into the darker ambiance of upcoming Good Friday. Either way, the readings designated for the rest of the Palm Sunday liturgy do tease us into a more reflective mood. We proclaim the story of Jesus' passion as retold in one of the Synoptic Gospels: Matthew, Mark, or Luke. And, throughout the first days of the coming week, beginning on this Sunday, we recall the oracles of the prophet Isaiah, known as the "Suffering Servant" songs.

These oracles, authored during the era of Israel's captivity in Babylon, have held significance for the Christian community since its inception, for they seemed to foretell Jesus' redemptive mission by linking his strange, suffering death with the coming messianic reign of justice and peace longingly awaited by the people of Israel. The servant songs are lyric with pathos, rich in suggestive imagery, and dense with dramatic passion.

> Behold my servant, whom I uphold,
>   my chosen, in whom my soul delights;
> I have put my Spirit upon my servant,

to bring forth justice to the nations;
not crying out or raising a voice,
    that it be heard in the street;
a bruised reed will not be broken,
    nor the dimly burning wick be quenched;
but justice will be faithfully brought forth.
For my servant will not fail or be discouraged
    till justice is established in all the earth.

Thus says the Most High,
    who created the heavens and stretched them out,
    who spread forth the earth and what comes from it,
who gives breath to the people upon it
    and spirit to those who walk in it:
"I am the Most High, I have called you in righteousness,
    I have taken you by the hand and kept you;
I have given you as a covenant to the people,
    a light to the nations,
    to open the eyes that are blind,
to bring out the prisoners from the dungeon,
    from the prison those who sit in darkness.
I am the Most High, that is my name;
    my glory I give to no other,
    nor my praise to graven images.
Behold, the former things have come to pass,
    and new things I now declare;
before they spring forth
    I tell you of them."

                                Isaiah 42:1-7

The words of the prophet establish Jesus as being with God from the beginning.

Listen to me, O coastlands,
    and hearken, you peoples from afar.
The Most High called me from the womb,
    from the body of my mother, God gave me a name.
My mouth was fashioned like a sharp sword,
    in the shadow of God's hand was I hidden;
made as a polished arrow,
    in God's own quiver was I hidden away.
And God said to me, "You are my servant,

Israel, in whom I will be glorified."
But I said, "I have labored in vain,
    I have spent my strength for nothing and vanity;
yet surely my right is with the Most High,
    and my recompense with my God."

And now you say, O God,
    who formed me from the womb to be your servant,
to bring Jacob back to you,
    and that Israel might be gathered to you,
for I am honored in your eyes, O God,
    and you have become my strength—
and so you say to me:
"It is too light a thing that you should be my servant
    to raise up the tribes of Jacob
    and to restore the preserved of Israel;
I will give you as a light to the nations,
    that my salvation may reach to the end of the earth."

Isaiah 49:1-6

And Jesus' identity as the Suffering Servant is made clear.

The Most High has given me
    the tongue of those well-taught,
that I may know how to sustain with a word
    those that are weary.
Morning by morning God wakens,
    God wakens my ear
    to hear as those who are taught.
The Most High has opened my ear,
    and I was not rebellious,
    I turned not backward.
I gave my back to the smiters,
    and my cheeks to those who pulled out the beard;
I hid not my face
    from shame and spitting.

For you, O God, help me;
    therefore I have not been confounded;
therefore I have set my face like a flint,
    and I know that I shall not be put to shame;
    The one who vindicates me is near.

Who will contend with me?
   Let us stand up together.
Who is my adversary?
   Let them come near to me.
Behold, the Most High God helps me;
   who will declare me guilty?
Behold, all of them will wear out like a garment;
   the moth will eat them up.

Isaiah 50:4-9

Atonement

We are at the threshold of the great week of the Atonement, the at-one-ment that takes place between ourselves and God. The doctrine of the atonement affirms that humanity is reconciled with God through Jesus the Christ and is central to Christian theology. However, there is no one normative articulation of the doctrine to be found anywhere in the wider Christian community. The canonical scriptures themselves offer a variety of metaphors describing the mystery that the early church asserted: that somehow Jesus Christ makes us one with God. The New Testament gives us language of sacrifice, of redemption, of victory, of reconciliation, and of revelation. It also locates the Atonement both in the fact of Jesus' death and in his resurrection. These central New Testament metaphors and understandings were expanded, modified, and creatively shaped in the centuries that followed by the living, praying community.

The cumulative spiritual tradition of the church thus provides us with a variety of perspectives on Christ's atoning activity which may enliven our collective reflections in the present. Perhaps the clearest way to introduce this plethora of insights into the atonement is to enumerate them in the negative rather than the positive.

For example, the Christ event does not only save us from our sins. It has been seen, by fair numbers of Christians, to do other things as well. The Christ event may make us victors over death and corruption. It may enable us to triumph over the powers of evil or darkness. It may liberate us from unjust structures and free us to begin to participate in the inbreaking reign of God. It may birth us into new life. It may bestow deification (God-likeness) upon us. It may usher in a new era and transform the cosmos itself. These are all familiar, yet somewhat alternate, ways of imaging the Christ event.

The point is this: it is not only the cross and the death that enable us to be at one with God. Creation itself as well as the incarnation and the life and the resurrection of Jesus have been focused upon as the defining, transforming features of the Christ event. For many Christians, it has been the entire process, the cycle of mysteries, that has been seized on as definitive.

Further, atonement (or salvation or redemption) is not necessarily a one-time event. The tradition for centuries assumed, and still often does, that becoming at one with God is an ongoing process in which we are called to participate. From the martyrs, who were believed to ascend immediately to the side of God upon their deaths and whose deaths were not uncommonly seen as continuing the victory over the powers that Christ's death began, to the monks who took up their own crosses in the ascetic form of poverty, chastity, and obedience, to the mystics whose intimate personal union with the divine life was a foretaste of the fullness Jesus promised, Christians for centuries saw the Christ event as ongoing in their lives. They were becoming more and more conformed to the God in whose image and likeness they were created by actively identifying with the God-man Jesus. This identification was quite often strikingly literal: a Francis of Assisi practicing a radical poverty that he felt was an emulation of the poor Christ, stripped on the cross; a Julian of Norwich asking to receive intimate knowledge of Christ's facing death through bodily suffering; a Thomas à Kempis recommending the practice of the virtues associated in his day with the Christ life; a John Wesley urging the practice of "going on to perfection."

This point is corollary to one other point: justification (God's acquittal, through Christ's sacrifice, of punishment due to humanity's sin) is not the only outcome Christians have perceived as issuing from the Christ event. Sanctification (growing participation in the holiness of Christ) and deification (humanity transfigured to divine life) are alternate or at least complementary models.

Next, seen from the wider tradition, the Atonement is not necessarily or primarily achieved for individuals but for the community. It is not only a personal experience, it is a cosmic event. If Jesus died for our sins, it has in the past been seen as much for our collective as for our personal salvation. The redeemed community was the focus of many earlier writers. Often creation itself and human history are understood to be transformed by the Christ event. One characteristic of Paul's view of atonement that deeply stamped the writing of the patristic era is his apocalyptic emphasis, the sense that Christ has led humanity into a new *eon*, which freed humanity from sin and death and led to new life. This wonderful, *cosmic* vision, which is more communal (at least for the community of the baptized) than individual, resonates in the thought of the church fathers.

Finally, the Atonement is not always conceived as the Father giving his Son nor as the Son being obedient to the Father. Much of the writing of the spiritual tradition avoids the latent tritheism of this model and is more clearly trinitarian in its tone. The second and first members are seen to be in relation to one another in a variety of ways. Often it is the second person who takes the initiative to give of self or it is the love, equally shared by all members of the Trinity, that is expressed in the Cross and Resurrection. Similarly, Jesus is not always depicted primarily as obedient Son. He appears in a vast variety of guises, some of his visages being ungendered. He is gardener, bridge, bed, fountain, mother, and friend, among many other things.

The wonderful result of delighting in the wide range of the tradition's images of prayer, vision, and reflection is that it can empower us to exercise our own imaginations. All of the reflection builds upon images of atonement found in the scriptures themselves.

This coming week will bring us the opportunity once again to engage in such theological reflection. But perhaps on the threshold of Holy Week we would best begin by what is the most widespread understanding of Atonement: that through his sacrificial death, Jesus substitutes for humankind, taking on himself the sins and thus the punishment due humanity for its sinfulness. Thus Jesus stands in our place so that our sins are not seen by God. Jesus bears them for us. This is the primary theology of those who name themselves "empty cross Christians." It is a perspective on the Atonement that might enrich the entire Christian community.

He Died for Me

Several years ago, just at the onset of the Gulf War, I found myself virtually unable to pray. It was a troubling time for the country and for me personally—a time of fear, anxiety, conflict, and tension. I had spent the previous decade involved in conscious efforts at peacemaking in both public and private spheres. This activity had taken place against the backdrop of a lifetime influenced by persons engaged in conscious efforts toward peace: a father who was a conscientious objector in World War II, contacts with the American Friends Service Committee and other Quaker groups, with clergy and laity of all denominations as well as secular groups throwing their energy behind ideas like "Peace is a word whose time has come." From the ban-the-bomb movement in the 1950s to the American Catholic bishops' statement on War and Peace in the 1980s, to Pax Christi, the International Catholic Peace Movement, from California to Massachusetts to Alabama to Wisconsin to Ohio to Nebraska, I had prayed, broken bread, and worked toward peace with innumerable brothers and sisters.

Thus, watching our nation slide inexorably toward war in January of 1991 (did no one else notice the irony that the day of reckoning—January 15—was Martin Luther King, Jr.'s birthday?) was for me an experience of spiritual hopelessness and vast sorrow, even despair.

The various religious communities of Omaha had banded together to pray for peace in the weeks preceding the outbreak of war. The Sunday after the announcement of war we were gathered, somewhat more bleakly than the week before, to pray now for a swift end to the swelling violence. Christians, Jews, and Muslims of various stripes—Baptist preachers, Unitarian spokespersons, Roman Catholic priests, Reformed rabbis, and the Imam of the local Sunni mosque—had led a thickly packed, fearful crowd gathered at St. Cecilia's cathedral in earnest prayers for some nonviolent solution to the crisis in the Persian Gulf.

I soon identified the source of my inability to pray. It was the experience of shame and immense grief that was my overwhelming emotion. Shame felt for us as a human community, myself included, swept over me. A powerful sense of the limitations and brokenness of us all stuck in my throat.

In my niche in the Christian tradition, the Roman communion, there exists a vital felt sense of the *possibility* of human growth and even, under ideal circumstances, perfection. Our Eastern Orthodox brothers and sisters hold an even more optimistic view of the human person and community. We do pray liturgically in the midst of the mass, "Lord, do not look at our sins but the faith of your church," but the overriding weight of our spiritual tradition causes our hearts to plead for our eventual perfection. So it is not an instinctive inner reflex for me to pray out of the sense of being unredeemable. Deep humility, woundedness, lostness, need—yes, these are familiar psychic qualities that emerge in prayer. But this felt experience of shame was different.

When I prayed, I was ashamed for God to look on us, on me, on the entire human condition which, while so clearly motivated by well-meaning, intelligent, faith-filled efforts, could not but resort to shameful violence.

I prayed and, to my astonishment, found myself asking Jesus to stand in front of me, of all of us, so that God might see the reality of his love and not our loveless failure. The generosity and beauty of his atoning act in the face of the horror we were creating was beyond words. This was a distinctly unfamiliar inner move, but nevertheless one which illuminated for me an experience cultivated in many Christian circles. He was substituting for me, for us, again.

Eat This Bread, Drink This Cup

In the fourth century, Christian pilgrims visiting Jerusalem began reenacting the last scenes of the life of Christ as liturgical drama during the ending days of Holy Week. Over the centuries the practice spread throughout Western and Eastern Christendom. Today Thursday, Friday, and Saturday are known as the Triduum Sacrum (sacred three days) and commemorate the Last Supper, Passion, and Death of Christ. These, together with Easter, are the most solemn and distinctive celebrations of the liturgical year.

The first of these sacred three days, Thursday, locates us around the time of the Jewish Passover in Jerusalem where Jesus and his disciples have gathered in an upper room. The events leading up to his impending arrest have already taken place. Religious officials, long suspicious of the rumors concerning this prophet-king from Nazareth, now have their suspect targeted. This rabble-rouser who seems to profane the sabbath and blaspheme against God has troubled them for some time. Jesus' arrival in Jerusalem has been duly noted, and the enthusiasm of the potentially subversive crowd that accompanied him has not escaped attention. Judas Iscariot has sought out the chief priests and offered to lead them to their target for the sum of thirty pieces of silver and is now waiting for an opportunity to betray his master. All of the Gospel narratives are heavy with a sense of impending doom. Jesus feels the precariousness of his position. Indeed, his highly visible entry into the city, with the climate of the city as tense as it was, could only have been made with Jesus fully conscious of the inflamatory consequences of such an act. He knows too that his present whereabouts will be made known to officials by one of his own number.

It is at this tense moment that Jesus enacts two distinctive gestures that will become symbolic of the entirety of his teaching and be ritually recapitulated over and over by Christian communities of succeeding generations. The gestures are at once utterly simple and profound, speaking, as only gestures can, more eloquently than the most polished words. He washes his friends' feet, and he shares a meal.

When You Eat This Bread

The two central gestures of the liturgy for Maundy Thursday are intimately connected. Both speak nonverbally of nurturing. I begin first with the gesture through which this is most obviously communicated.

> [The] Lord Jesus on the night when he was betrayed took bread, and when he had given thanks, he broke it, and said, "This is my body which is for you. Do this in remembrance of me." In the same way also the cup, after supper, saying, "This cup is the new covenant in my blood. Do this, as often as you drink it, in remembrance of me."
>
> 1 Corinthians 11:23-25

To break bread and pass the cup became, for the earliest Christians, the ritual gesture that defined who they were. They were a thanksgiving (eucharist) people, in communion with one another through their sharing of the bread and cup that was the body and blood of Christ. Over the centuries Christians have refined their various precise definitions of this ritual, even separating themselves from one another over their differing formulations. Yet to me, the spare gesture itself, powerful and telling in its simplicity, transcends all divisions.

The simple phrases of the American folk hymn sings the deepest meaning of the gesture.

> *Let us break bread together on our knees;*
> *Let us break bread together on our knees;*
> *When I fall on my knees,*
> *With my face to the rising sun,*
> *O Lord, have mercy on me.*
>
> *Let us drink wine together on our knees;*
> *Let us drink wine together on our knees;*
> *When I fall on my knees,*
> *With my face to the rising sun,*
> *O Lord, have mercy on me.*[22]

At its most elemental level, the gesture proclaims Christianity as a community of mutual need and nourishment whose very life, at all its levels, is sustained by its continuous feeding of one another and being fed, a nurturant symbiosis constantly replenished by the nourishment of Christ's own sustenance.

That Christ is the ultimate source of nourishment for the community of faith is a recurrent theme of medieval Christianity. The High Middle Ages was a period of intense eucharistic devotion with a flair for envisioning the communion of divine/human eating and drinking in a highly physical manner. The literal eating of the body and blood of Christ became the subject for prayerful reflection (this, of course, accords with the theology of the period).

In this context, Christ became for Christians the equivalent of a nursing mother, one who fed her children from her own substance. In the associative imagery of contemplative prayer, the wounds pierced in his side became the breasts from which the infant Christian was fed. (This accorded with medieval physiology which taught that breastmilk was reconstituted from a woman's blood.) Jesus was thus our mother, tenderly embracing and feeding us from his own breast. Among many medieval spiritual writers who utilized the imagery of Jesus as mother is Catherine of Siena, fourteenth-century Italian holy woman. Catherine herself was the recipient of a vision in which she met the wounded Christ who gently placed his hand upon her neck (as would a mother with a nursing baby) and drew her to his open side, encouraging her to drink from the fountain of life. The visionary corresponded with numerous persons who sought her advice on spiritual matters. To three women of Naples she wrote:

> Dearest mother and sisters in sweet Jesus Christ, I Catherine . . . write to you in his precious blood, with the desire to see you confirmed in true and perfect charity so that you be true nurses of your souls. For we cannot nourish others if first we do not nourish our own souls with true and real virtues. . . . Do as the child does who, wanting to take milk, takes the mother's breast and places it in his mouth and draws to himself the milk by means of the flesh. So . . . we must attach ourselves to the breast of the crucified Christ, in whom we find the mother of charity, and draw from there by means of his flesh (that is the humanity) the milk that nourishes our soul.[23]

Holy Thursday is the day on which the Christian community in a special way celebrates Christ's maternal nurturance. It is also the day on which we are enjoined to nurture one another, to love as we have been loved. With a mother's tender love we are entrusted to each other. We eat from the same table. We drink from the same cup. We give to each other from our own substance. We, in turn, are fed by one another. The sharing we do in the church, the body of Christ, is more than fellowship, more than working side by side. We share in a profound communion at the root of our beings, on levels only dimly accessible to consciousness. We are lives interconnected at the core. Flowing from the same spring, the waters of divine life pulse through each of our beings, joining us as tributaries angling off from a single waterway.

We are mothers to one another, carrying each other beneath our hearts, slinging one another high on waiting hips when the walking becomes too difficult, lifting our hands behind each others' necks to bring hungry mouths to feed, giving our own substance to bring each other life.

A New Command

The meal that Jesus institutes at the Last Supper is at once a sign of our mutual nourishment and a reenactment of his own nurturance. In the Gospel of John the significance of this twofold meaning is underscored. John's description of the Last Supper is the most extended and theologically rich of the Gospel accounts. Aware of his impending death, Jesus lingers with his friends, passing on to them the loving words that he wishes them to remember, enjoining them to the coming tasks they must face without having him in the same way he has been with them, entrusting them to one another, promising them that his spirit will always be there to support and comfort. At the outset of this solicitude, he performs an action which he then interprets as a "new command":

> Before the feast of the Passover, when Jesus knew that his hour had come to depart out of this world to the One who had sent him, having loved his own who were in the world, he loved them to the end. During supper, when the devil had already put it into the heart of Judas Iscariot, Simon's son, to betray him, Jesus, knowing that God had given all things into his hands, and that he had come from God and was going to God, rose from supper, laid aside his garments, and girded himself with a towel. Then he poured water into a basin, and began to wash the feet of his companions, and to wipe them with the towel with which he was girded. He came to Simon Peter; and Peter said to him, "Lord, do you wash my feet?" Jesus answered him, "What I am doing you do not know now, but afterward you will understand." Peter said to him, "You shall never wash my feet." Jesus answered him, "If I do not wash you, you have no part in me." Simon Peter said to him, "Lord, not my feet only

but also my hands and my head!" Jesus said to him, "The one who bathes needs only to wash the feet to be clean all over; and you are clean, but not every one of you." For he knew who was to betray him; that was why he said, "You are not all clean."

When he had washed their feet, and taken his garments, and resumed his place, he said to them, "Do you know what I have done to you? You call me Teacher and Lord; and you are right, for so I am. If I then, your Lord and Teacher, have washed your feet, you also ought to wash one another's feet. For I have given you an example, that you also should do as I have done to you.

John 13:1-15

I give you a new commandment: love one another; you must love one another just as I have loved you. It is by your love for one another, that everyone will recognise you as my disciples.

John 13:34-35, NJB

The title of the feast day, Maundy Thursday, was popularized in England. It refers to this command and the gesture that expresses it. *Mandatum novum* (new command) is the Latin phrase used in the traditional antiphon that accompanies the ceremony of foot washing particular to this liturgy.

Not all denominations observe Holy Thursday with a ritual of foot washing. While the liturgical practice has long roots in the tradition, the ceremony itself has been variously placed throughout the centuries, at times finding its way into the Holy Thursday service proper, at times placed as a separate service observed at a different hour during the day.

Be this as it may, the foot washing is a wonderfully pregnant ritual, full of import for the day in which our mutuality is so much in focus. The ceremony is typically accomplished by having the ordained presider kneel before twelve persons (who represent the disciples gathered at the Last Supper) and wash and dry their feet in a small basin. As it was for Peter in the Johannine account, the gesture (which is one of startling reversal) surprises and jolts one into thinking things out anew. The one to whom we tend to look for leadership and in whom we invest authority is seen kneeling and tenderly serving. In the gospel account Jesus is quite explicit about the gesture's meaning. This is a new command. Love a new way. Love by caretaking. Love by being available to one another. Love by serving. In a world which clamors for status and recognition, this is a countercultural statement.

Again, there is something strikingly maternal about kneeling and washing. I say this with some hesitation because I think it is too easy for "service equals women" to become a way to continue to reinforce the idea that men will not or cannot be counted on to be nurturing, compassionate, or otherwise get their hands dirty. It also justifies keeping women confined to the domestic sphere mantled in the ideology of loving Christian devotion. My keenest insight into the gesture that Jesus enacts among his friends is that we are all enjoined to compassionate nurturance of one another, in all circumstances. Our caretaking cannot be tidily domesticated and relegated to the safe haven of home, thereby creating a dichotomy between public and private spheres with women presiding in publically irrelevant occupations (except through their children). Maternal nurturance cannot be confined to one gender or simply to the activity of childrearing, as essential as that is. It must, rather, be the concern of us all.[24]

Deeper into the Mystery

The liturgical mood of Holy Thursday is complex. It begins with grandeur. White vestments, which have not been displayed since the beginning of Lent, visually anticipate the triumph of Easter. The sounds of the choir singing the Gloria, absent from our celebration for some time, now fill the air. In some denominations the festival mood is marked by reclaiming the ancient custom of granting absolution to the congregation to mark the end of the penitential season begun on Ash Wednesday. Always the Old Testament story of the institution of the Passover feast is read, thus calling to mind the grand scheme of salvation history. We recall how the Israelites in Egypt sacrificed lambs and smeared their doorpost lintels with blood so that their homes would be passed over and no plague would harm them (Exod. 12:1-14). The Christian community has in hindsight read this text as a foreshadowing of the sacrifice of Jesus that will, in its time, cause God to "pass over" our sins. Thus the feast of the Passover with its promise of liberation is fresh in our minds. We link the Last Supper with the feast as do the Gospels of Matthew, Mark, and Luke (John indicates that the upper room event took place before the actual Passover). The hope of the coming liberation of Easter hovers in the air. It is thus not uncommon for Christians to gather in a spirit of festivity for a supper or an actual Passover seder.

Yet quickly enough the mood shifts as the liturgy moves to its conclusion. The momentum of the Passion story asserts itself and we find ourselves aware of the coming, dark events, the necessary descent before the rising. We move, as it were, into the garden with Jesus where he retires and waits. We, like the disciples with whom he pleads to remain, watch and pray.

Traditionally, the Maundy Thursday service has no closure. We leave the church unaccompanied by music or benediction or blessing. The altar is stripped of the celebrative dressing. The church is left stark and bare. We hear the footfalls echo as we leave in silence. In denominations in which the eucharist is central, the host is carried in procession to a side chapel there to be reserved until Easter vigil. We are silent. We wait. We keep watch. We hope.

our love will carry us through the next few days.

Eating - the meal - messy business - just like being in community & working to love one another.

We can't mess up the meal - as long as we are doing it in loving remembrance of Jesus for our community.

It is through love that we are recognized & upheld.

Freely Flowing

In the worldwide Roman communion there is only one day of the entire year during which the eucharistic liturgy is not celebrated. That day is Good Friday. The altars of churches everywhere are bare. On their knees before flickering votive lights, in silent chapels, people keep vigil throughout the dark night that leads into the most solemn day of the Christian calendar.

We bore deeper into the mystery of dying and being born. We keep in mind and heart the account of Jesus' last day as variously recorded in Matthew, Mark, and Luke. Half identifying ourselves with Jesus who agonizes in the garden, alert with anticipation of the inevitable arrest that awaits him, we also discover ourselves in his disciples who gather at the far end of the garden. He has asked us to stay awake and pray. Sleepy and oblivious of the ominous chain of events already set in motion, we stumble into the yawning cavern of imminent death.

The Greek-born Spanish mannerist artist El Greco painted Christ's agony at Gethsemane in the turbulent, elongated style that was his trademark. The figure of Jesus dominates the painter's canvas. He kneels in the center, his gaze arched to the right, body raised in restless motion. Above him, meeting his gaze, hovers a winged messenger, a chalice clasped in her outstretched hand. The two seem inexorably drawn together by some magnetic force. Behind them a surreal landscape swirls, clouds and rocks alike press inward on either side, framing their meeting with gathering energy. To Jesus' right, and beneath the angel messenger in a sweeping circle of rock, the disciples are heaped upon one another, slumbering in oblivion. The restive, emotive tension of El Greco's brushwork well suits the drama of the scene.

We do embark on a day of the highest drama. We read from the Gospel of John:

> Jesus went forth with his companions across Kidron valley, where there was a garden, which he and his companions entered. Now Judas, who betrayed him, also knew the place; for Jesus often met there with them. So Judas, procuring a band of soldiers and some officers from the religious authorities, went there with lanterns and

torches and weapons. Jesus, knowing all that was to befall him, came forward and said to them, "Whom do you seek?" They answered him, "Jesus of Nazareth." Jesus said to them, "I am he." Judas, who betrayed him, was standing with them. When he said to them, "I am he," they drew back and fell to the ground. Again he asked them, "Whom do you seek?" And they said, "Jesus of Nazareth." Jesus answered, "I told you that I am he; so, if you seek me, let these others go." This was to fulfill the word which he had spoken, "Of those whom you gave me I lost not one." Then Simon Peter, having a sword, drew it and struck the high priest's slave and cut off his ear. The slave's name was Malchus. Jesus said to Peter, "Put your sword into its sheath; shall I not drink the cup which I have been given to drink?"

So the band of soldiers and their captain and the officers of the temple seized Jesus and bound him.

John 18:1-12

Time is foreshadowed as events pile up on one another. Jesus is led to Annas, an official of the Jewish council, who sends him to the high priest Caiaphas, who in turn sends him to the Roman court of Pilate. There Jesus' fate is sealed.

Then Pilate took Jesus and scourged him. The soldiers plaited a crown of thorns, and put it on his head, and arrayed him in a purple robe; they came up to him, saying, "Hail, King of the Jews!" and struck him with their hands. Pilate went out again, and said to them, "See, I am bringing him out to you, that you may know that I find no crime in him." So Jesus came out, wearing the crown of thorns and the purple robe. Pilate said to them, "Behold the man!" When the religious authorities and the officers saw him, they cried out, "Crucify him, crucify him!" Pilate said to them, "Take him yourselves and crucify him, for I find no crime in him." They answered him, "We have a law, and by that law he ought to die, because he has made himself the Chosen One of God." When Pilate heard these words, he was the more afraid; he entered the praetorium again and said to Jesus, "Where are you from?" But Jesus gave no answer. Pilate therefore said to him, "You will not speak to me? Do you not know that I have power to release you, and power to crucify you?" Jesus answered him, "You would have no power over me unless it had been given you from above; therefore those who delivered me to you have the greater sin."

Upon this Pilate sought to release him, but they cried out, "If you release this man, you are not Caesar's friend; every one who makes himself a king sets himself against Caesar." When Pilate heard these words, he brought Jesus out and sat down on the judgment seat at a place called The Pavement, and in Hebrew, Gabbatha. Now it was the day of Preparation of the Passover; it was about the sixth hour. He said to them, "Behold your King!" They cried out, "Away with him, away with him, crucify him!" Pilate said to them, "Shall I crucify your King?" The religious authorities answered, "We have no king but Caesar." Then he handed Jesus over to them to be crucified.

So they took Jesus, and he went out, bearing his own cross, to the place called the place of a skull, which is called in Hebrew Golgotha. There they crucified him, and with him two others, one on either side, and Jesus between them. Pilate also wrote a title and put it on the cross; it read, "Jesus of Nazareth, the King of the Jews." Many read this title, for the place where Jesus was crucified was near the city; and it was written in Hebrew, in Latin, and in Greek. The religious leaders said to Pilate, "Do not write, 'The King of the Jews', but, 'This man said, I am King of the Jews.'" Pilate answered, "What I have written I have written."

When the soldiers had crucified Jesus they took his garments and made four parts, one for each soldier; also his tunic. But the tunic was without seam, woven from top to bottom; so they said to one another, "Let us not tear it, but cast lots for it to see whose it shall be." This was to fulfill the scripture, "They parted my garments among them, and for my clothing they cast lots."

So the soldiers did this. But standing by the cross of Jesus were his mother, and his mother's sister, Mary the wife of Clopas, and Mary Magdalene. When Jesus saw his mother and the disciple whom he loved standing near, he said to his mother, "Woman, behold, your son!" Then he said to the disciple, "Behold, your mother!" And from that hour the disciple took her to his own home.

After this Jesus, knowing that all was now finished, said (to fulfill the scripture), "I thirst." A bowl full of vinegar stood there; so they put a sponge full of the vinegar on hyssop and held it to his mouth. When Jesus had received the vinegar, he said, "It is finished"; and he bowed his head and gave up his spirit.

John 19:1-30

The Last Words

Western tradition has focused intently upon the final episodes of Jesus' life. The greater the proximity to the crucifixion itself, so crucial to

Western Christendom's understanding of redemption, the keener the focus. Thus, Jesus' last words and final recorded gestures are of great significance. Perhaps this is what we do with all those who die. We search through the shards left by the ones who have passed over because we are both drawn to and repelled by the mystery of dying. We seem to feel that if we puzzle and turn over the artifacts uncovered in the median realm between life and death, we will touch something of another life. Last moments, last words seem a lens through which we finally view clearly the qualities distilled through a lifetime. We hold in veneration the sacred space of time which opens out into the gateway of our passing through.

I know this to be true of my own father's dying. He had been ill for a long time, so death was not unanticipated. But the actual end came quite unexpectedly. With pulmonary fibrosis, a degenerative lung disease, breathing becomes more and more difficult. Gradually the other vital capacities, all of which require breath, suffer and give way. Each time my mother phoned with news of a new complication, I wondered if this was the entryway into the end. Because we live halfway across the country, I wanted to be informed of all emergencies so that I could make plans to fly out if need be. When she called midweek in late February to say that speech was becoming difficult, I wondered this again. But a phone call to the pulmonologist, who was the medical specialist on the case, gave no cause for immediate alarm. The end was no doubt within sight in the next few months he informed me, but certainly not imminent. My mother, in her blessedly intuitive way, met the present crisis by suggesting that we contact a friend of mine who is an Episcopal priest. Several months before, in the anxiety of long-distance caretaking, I had phoned my friend and asked if she would mind paying my folks a visit since she lived nearby. They had not sought out an explicitly spiritual companion to be present to them during those hard days, and I suggested my priest friend might be a help to them. They were open to the suggestion and her pastoral visit had meant a great deal to them both, especially my father, who seemed to be courageously coping with his gradual debilitation out of the reserves he had stored up in that pastoral session. So to see if she could come once again seemed an excellent idea. Although my father at first dismissed the suggestion on the grounds that my friend was undoubtedly too busy, I called and discovered that she did have time and would be delighted to pay a call.

As she recounted to me later, she arrived in the early afternoon and had the overwhelming sense that she was present to someone in the fragile liminal space between life and death. He was alert, laboring to breathe, but in the full possession of his mental faculties. They spoke briefly (he could not sustain a sentence). She asked if he was comfortable with a ritual of anointing (all his life he had been critical of institutional and ritual religion). He was. Symbolic gestures do create passageways that make significant human transitions possible. She anointed him. Then she told him that it was all right to let go. He told her to tell me that he loved me.

The entire exchange was brief and simple but consoling. Later that day I phoned my mother before going out to dinner and she seemed calmed by the visit. The assisting nurse who had recently been hired to spell her during the night hours was about to arrive and she was grateful to be settling down for a restful evening. When I arrived home several hours later the babysitter announced that my mother had phoned with the news that my dad had died. She had left the room to go eat dinner and he had simply let go. It is strange how the specifics of the last moments, the last hour, the last day are so significant. My father died beautifully, with a grace and simplicity that astonish me. Yet his prolonged dying over the previous years had been agonizing.

We are instinctively drawn to the temporal threshold of death and fix upon the words, the gestures, the atmosphere that hovers there with wonder. They hold significance as if they had been suspended in time and space. They lead us into the centers of silence within which our deepest questions lie. This profound inward drawing is, I think, what compels us to linger at the foot of the cross and to memorize the last utterances of Jesus.

The Christian tradition has distilled his final moments for us as the "Seven Last Words." Over the years, theologians and biblical exegetes have written extensively on the last utterances recorded in the Gospels. And composers have translated the final words into the medium of music. Among them Joseph Haydn, at the turn of the eighteenth century, attempted to express the various emotional tonalities of the last words in purely instrumental form. Haydn was commissioned to compose his "Seven Last Words" by a Spanish churchman for performance in the Cathedral of Cádez on Good Friday. Scored for a small orchestra, the composition begins with an introduction in which the poignant delicacy of the violin passages are played against passages of more orchestral massiveness that set the stage for the emotional range of the piece. In the interpretation of Luke 23:34, "Father, forgive them; for they know not what they do," Haydn employs a slow tempo, while a graceful yielding melody creates a mood of calm acceptance. "Today shalt thou be with me in paradise" (Luke 23:43) receives a marking of "Grave and Cantabile," which reflects the majestic and expansive mood of the second sonata. Even more solemn and intimate is the opening response to John 19:26ff, "Woman, behold thy son! . . . behold thy mother!" As the segment continues, the juxtaposition of violin voices captures the sensitive action occurring between John the beloved disciple and Mary the mother. The anguish of Jesus' cry "Eli, Eli, lama sabachthani?"—"My God, my God, why hast thou forsaken me?" (Matt. 27:46; Mark 15:34) is captured in the surging melodies of the composition's fourth sonata. A more agitated rhythm created by plucking and muting the strings interprets "I thirst" (John 19:28). "It is finished" (John 19:30) brings forth a more lyric mood, while "Into thy hands I commend my spirit" (Luke 23:46) returns us to the slow tempo of the opening sonata. The entire composition closes with a final section of descriptive music entitled "The Earthquake" which employs trumpets and kettledrums to recreate the upheaval of nature occasioned by the death of the Son of God.

Haydn's piece was originally performed at a Tre Ore (Three Hours) service, a familiar devotional practice that persists to the present day. From noon to three P.M. on Good Friday a church may present a program of sermons based on the seven last words. Interspersed with musical interludes, the seven sermons expand on the themes of the words, plumbing the theological and spiritual depths discovered there.

On occasion, such services may become didactic opportunities for presiders who feel responsible to instruct as well as edify, to define precisely for their listeners what official teaching proclaims to be the significance of this mystery we celebrate. But our true hunger, I think, is to kneel not only before the mystery of this one death, but to kneel before death itself, to bring our fear, our longing, and the stubbornly seeded hopes of our broken lives to the threshold where we will each, in our own turn, cross over. There we hunger to find God. And perhaps, as we gaze at the broken, painracked human body, we might see in that pain, as through a window, a tender presence that can render such brokenness transparent. Then our own pain might become as well a window translucent with light.

The Blood and Waters of Birth

In the English city of Norwich during the turbulent, war-torn, plague-racked fourteenth century, a recluse by the name of Julian received a series of visions or "showings" of the crucified Christ. Many contemplatives in the Christian tradition before her had made it a practice to meditate upon the Lord as he underwent his passion, and many before her had recounted that the same cross hung Lord had appeared to them in extraordinary ways. To receive such a vision was to know salvation from the inside. A vision was a participation in the dynamic of redemption itself. But even among visionary accounts, Julian's revelations are especially rich. In part, this is because after experiencing them in a painracked state in which those present deemed her to be dying, she hid the visions in her heart and prayed with them for twenty years. The result was that she came to comprehend the meaning implicit in the imagery in a deep and expanded way.

Julian developed the theme, already present in the spiritual tradition, of the motherhood of Christ in a manner that went far beyond her predecessors. For Julian, Christ is our mother both in nature and in grace, the former because he is the foundation of our own natural creation and the latter because he took on our created nature. Thirdly, Christ is motherhood at work and so "everything is penetrated, in length and in breadth, in height and in depth without end; and it is all one love."[25] By feeding us with himself and by bearing us for life, Christ does this work of mothering.

> The mother's service is nearest, readiest and surest: nearest because it is most natural, readiest because it is most loving, and surest because it is truest. No one ever might or could perform this office fully, except only him. We know that all our mothers bear us for pain and death. O, what is that? But our true Mother Jesus, he alone bears us for joy and for endless life, blessed may he be. So he carries us within him in love and travail, until the full time when he wanted to suffer the sharpest thorns and cruel pains that ever were or will be, and at the last he died. And when he had finished, and had borne us so, for bliss, still all this could not satisfy his wonderful love. And he revealed this in these a great surpassing words of love [heard in Shewings]: If I could suffer more, I would suffer more. He could not die any more, but he did not want to cease working; therefore he must needs nourish us, for the precious love of motherhood has made him our debtor.[26]

In pain, amid the waters and blood of birth, we are born to new life through the body of Jesus our mother. Our God is a God of infinite nurturing love who carries us beneath the heart, who is stretched by our growing, with whose being we are so intimate that we are folded within. This God labors so that we might emerge, gasping, into newness of life.

Christians have marveled in myriad ways over this nearly incomprehensible truth: that somehow we are made one with God through God's own graceful inclination. Through God's own dying we are born. And for centuries Christians, especially in the western church, have experienced the blood of that birthing as cleansing, healing, and restoring. The blood of birth washes us clean. Linked to the idea of sacrifice and the sacred offering performed to reconcile humanity with divinity, blood is a powerful symbol in our tradition.

Another one of my favorite metaphors from the medieval tradition that probes the mystery of Christ's blood and extends its meaning beyond the idea of healing or sacrifice is the metaphor of Christ the winepress. Here again, although not explicitly a metaphor of mothering, the winepress expresses God's nurturance. It was not unusual in church architecture or in illuminated manuscripts to see Jesus portrayed on the cross surrounded by trailing vines heavy with grapes. The cross became the winepress, his body the fruit-heavy vine crushed to extract the wine that then slacked the thirst of a parched, God-yearning humankind.

The startling physicality of medieval devotion might alarm our modern, spiritualized sensibilities, which shy away from notions such as eating and drinking God. But the images often pry open our dulled perceptions and allow us to see into these inexhaustible mysteries with innocent eyes and vulnerable hearts. Such, for me, are the images of Catherine of Siena, fourteenth-century Italian mystic and prophetess whose prayerful images of the passion give us access to depths of meaning encoded in this event. The following prayer Catherine wrote on Passion Sunday, 1379.

> It was in this Word's Passion that
> . . . .
> the fire hidden under our ashes
> began to show itself
> completely and generously
> by splitting open his most holy body

on the wood of the cross.
And it was to draw the soul's affection
to high things,
and to bring the mind's eye
to gaze into the fire,
that your eternal Word
wanted to be lifted up high.
From there you have shown us love
in your blood,
and in your blood
you have shown us your mercy
and generosity.
In this blood
you have shown how our sin weighs you down.
In this blood
you have washed the face of your spouse, the soul,
with whom you are joined
by the union of the divine nature
with our human nature.
In this blood you clothed her
when she was naked,
and by your death
you restored her to life.
. . . .
O agreeable, peaceful Passion!
You make the soul sail on
in tranquil peace
over the waves of the stormy sea!
O delightful, so sweet Passion!
O wealth of the soul!
O refreshment for the troubled!
O food for the famished!
O gate and paradise for the soul!
O true gladness!
O our glory and blessedness!
The soul who glories in you
discovers her fruitfulness.[27]

At the Foot of the Cross

My eldest daughter calls it the "tremble, tremble song." The spare lyrics
and the haunting melody of the Afro-American spiritual, like the

surprising images of medieval devotion, can pry open our distracted hearts. They can lead us to the silent, windswept hill where the grieving remnant huddles in the shadow of the cross. There we locate ourselves in the narrative. The ghoulish crowds of onlookers drawn by the grotesque delight of viewing a pain-racked death have long since disappeared. The searing drama is finished. We are emptied of knowing and hoping. We wait.

> *Were you there when they crucified my Lord?*
> *Were you there when they crucified my Lord?*
> *O! Sometimes it causes me to tremble, tremble, tremble,*
> *Were you there when they crucified my Lord?*
>
> *Were you there when they nailed him to the tree?*
> *Were you there when they nailed him to the tree?*
> *O! Sometimes it causes me to tremble, tremble, tremble,*
> *Were you there when they nailed him to the tree?*
>
> *Were you there when they pierced him in the side?*
> *Were you there when they pierced him in the side?*
> *O! Sometimes it causes me to tremble, tremble, tremble*
> *Were you there when they pierced him in the side?*[28]

The church remembers the still solemnity of this dark and fecund moment through its ritual of the veneration of the cross. It kneels before the mystery of death. It bows before the threshold beyond which none of us has yet ventured and through which each of us yet must pass. It is humbled before the breadth, length, depth, and height of the love offered to it there.

The Roman communion incorporates the veneration of the cross into its Good Friday service. Typically, the presider and assistants process from the back of the church carrying the crucifix in silence and with great solemnity. Three times they stop while the presider chants the refrain:

> Behold, behold the wood of the cross on which is hung our salvation; oh come, let us adore.

The procession moves to the front of the church where the congregation is invited to come forward and individually venerate the cross. At the parish where we presently worship, a life-sized cross made of unhewn tree limbs is carried forward by the present year's catechumens (new members to be initiated into the church) and supported by them in front of the altar while worshipers kneel, bow, kiss, or in some way acknowledge the cross.

The first time I ever participated in a veneration service was in the early 1970s, the year before I was formally confirmed in the Roman Catholic Church. My upbringing had been religiously eclectic but primarily Protestant, and so I had no childhood readiness for a ritual such as the veneration of the cross. The Catholic church nearest to my home at the time was in a predominantly Spanish-speaking neighborhood. At midday on Good Friday I found myself in the pews at Our Lady of Sorrows sitting next to a group of elderly Hispanic women wearing black lace mantillas and shawls, bowed on their kneelers in deep absorption. If I had been to a midday Good Friday service previously, it had been at the Catholic church further uptown in an Anglo neighborhood where the seven last words were the focus of the celebration. There the veneration of the cross had been a discreet head-bobbing acknowledgment of an elegant gold crucifix elevated by the priest. But here in the dim and cavernous depths of Our Lady of Sorrows, I sensed a different mood, one for which I was not altogether prepared. The aesthetic of Spanish Catholicism is one of intense emotional extremes. A Spanish crucifix is likely to portray the dying savior in the most graphic extremity of his pain, blood flowing freely and copiously from his wounds, his tortured body slumped grotesquely forward.

The extended service had been going on for some time when we entered the ritual of the veneration. The voice of the presider suddenly boomed out from the back of the church: "Behold, behold, the wood of the cross!" Startled, I turned and found myself confronted with the oncoming specter of a writhing, blood-soaked Jesus held aloft by a dark-haired, olive-skinned altar boy. The dark-mantled women around me seemed drawn deeper into their ecstatic reveries. As the crucifix passed by they did not simply genuflect, they sank to the ground in profound adoration. Uncomfortably I too knelt, confused as to what was expected of me next and uneasy with the deep inclining going on around me. I had never been taught to really kneel, never been expected, through the language of the body, to learn the art of inclining the heart. This prostration of the whole self, this kinesthetic acknowledgment of my indebtedness, this bodily reverencing of the love that cannot be fully grasped was outside my experience. I towered above these graciously receptive women, stiff and unyielding in this unfamiliar spiritual attitude.

Then to my consternation, we rose and began to file out of our pews toward the front of the church where we were to kneel at the altar rail and kiss the cross as it was presented to us. I shrank back interiorly but kept moving forward in the line of mantillas and shawls. Soon I found myself kneeling, pressed close between the worshippers on either side of me. To my left was an ancient, bent woman, her face lost in the folds of her black mantilla. I was keenly aware of the vast distance between us created by our different experiences. She elderly, I young; she no doubt only semi-literate, possibly unfamiliar with the dominant language of our culture, I a graduate student, one of the elitely literate of our society; she poor, I the product of economic comfort; her world extending perhaps no farther than the immediate circle of her kin, mine being the wide world of national and international academia; her work that of maternal caretaking or perhaps the drudgery of domestic service, mine the sometimes self-preoccupied and privileged work of ideas. I felt desperately out of place and wished I were anywhere else.

Then I saw our hands. They were placed side by side on the padded railing, each a silent statement of our respective lives. One aging and marred by lack of care, one youthful and pampered. Yet as the crucifix approached above our downturned heads and we surrendered ourselves to its mystery, the differences of our hands dissolved in my perception. They were not two different hands but one, made so by the unspeakable graciousness of the divine love that inclined toward us. My hand, my self, was the same hand and the same self bowed to my left. At the foot of the cross all alike are nourished, all are washed by the blood that flows so freely.

Laid in the Earth

On the campus of the Catholic university where I teach is a meditation garden familiarly called "The Jesuit Garden" because it is nestled behind the historic residence of the Jesuit priests who were the university's first educators. Today, a new apartment module that houses a portion of the present Jesuit population flanks the gardens on the east. The garden is situated at the highest point of the campus and provides an overlook of a portion of the downtown area of the central city.

Set well apart from the heavily traveled central walkways of the inner-city campus, the garden provides a space of contemplative refuge that invites a reflective stroll or a solitary prayer. Much of the garden consists of an irregular oval lawn, dotted with trees, around which a path meanders. But at the garden's west side, in what I assume is its oldest portion, is a circular stone courtyard encircled by bushes whose visual focal point is an earth mound. Atop the mound sits an ancient observatory and into its base is carved a rock grotto.

Sitting on one of the wooden benches encircling the courtyard, one can gaze out over the city in the near distance. But a more natural focus is to become attentive to the garden, the grotto, and the observatory. It is not infrequent, in architectural products of late nineteenth and early twentieth century Catholicism, to find somewhere a grotto in which is placed a shrine to the Virgin Mary. The Jesuit gardens are no exception. Long ago builders hollowed out the side of the small hillock and fashioned a rocky inset into which they placed a statue of Mary. The grotto in the Jesuit garden, although it contains running water only part of the year, appears to be the nurturant source of the banked flower beds that surround the stone courtyard. Plants and shrubs of many varieties, playfully spontaneous in their arrangement, seem watered by the same source. It is a celebration of earth's capacity for bringing forth life.

Grottos are wonderful places. I think of them as moist, intimate spaces celebrating the inner recesses of the earth. They are archetypally and frankly female, giving us spatial access to some only dimly grasped mystery of earth and spirit and dying and being born. Among grottos, the one in the Jesuit gardens is unique because of the observatory atop the hillock into which the rocks are set. It was the sky laboratory of one of the university's early Jesuit scientists for whom the modern science complex is now named. During the early years of this century the priest-scientist searched the stars of the nighttime sky from the interior of the small silver dome atop the hillock in the gardens. He scanned the heavens, casting a long glance that anchored the aspirations of earth in the deep sea of the heavens. He was part of a religious order founded in the sixteenth century, embued with the ethos of that era of global exploration, humanism, and scientific discovery. Jesuits have been fervent missionaries who found themselves captivated by the cultures they came to convert. They have been ardent investigators of the biological wonders of creation and eager advocates of human rights. They have been spiritual men who looked first to the created order to find God. The ethos of their founding age led them to explore the human heart as the place of intersection of human and divine desire. The Jesuits, born in an age of Christian humanism, intuit as their birthright the connection between heaven and earth.

It is Holy Saturday and I come to the Jesuit garden where the eye and the heart are drawn out and upward by the silver dome of the now-unused observatory and down and inward by the rocky recesses of the Marian grotto.

During the weeks of Lent I have seen the garden in different moods. Most of the time it has been too cold to linger on one of the benches; a quick passage through, huddled in a down jacket, has been the most that could be expected. The flower beds have been empty; only a few evergreen trees and a hardy perennial bush or two have added a hint of green to the brown and grey of the winter palette. Now the earth's color hidden mysteriously from view is beginning to show itself. The first shoots of the daffodils poke out of the ground. In a sunny section of the courtyard, their neon-yellow petals attract the eye. The first blossoms of the gnarled pear tree show themselves white against the black bark. The lilacs, heavy with virgin green leaves, promise their purple festoons. The winter earth gives birth to the springtime miracle of new life.

The Day of the Earth

Like the observatory and the grotto of the Jesuit gardens, the pictorial tradition of western Christendom leads our imagination down from the heights of the cross to the depths of the earth. Artists for centuries have been fond of painting, sculpting, and carving representations of Jesus' descent from the cross, the *pieta* (his mother bearing him in her arms), and the entombment. Christ's descending into the depths of the earth has thus been lovingly reproduced for the edification of generations of worshippers. One of my favorite renderings of one moment of this process is done by Giotto di Bondone, the early Renaissance Italian artist famous for his fresco technique and for the fresh, naturalistic, and psychologically expressive treatment of his subjects. Giotto's *Lamentation*, which is part of a fresco cycle in the Arena Chapel at Padua, finds us in the circle of mourning followers who have received the body of their broken Lord. Christ's reclining form is clutched in the arms of a passionate Mary Magdalene. Other figures cluster about him, sitting, kneeling, or standing, each captured in a grief distinctive to his or her self. John, the beloved disciple, leans toward his master with arms flung back away from his chest as if he wished to swoop down upon the body but is restrained by the finality of death. Mary stands at her son's head, mantled from head to toe in a blue drape, her hands clutched together beneath her cheek, her pain drawing her deeper into the folds of her cloak. In the sky above, a consort of tiny angels arches and writhes in the agony of sorrow. The intimacy of the captured moment is unforgettable. His friends prepare to release their loved one to the arms of the earth.

> Since it was the day of Preparation, in order to prevent the bodies from remaining on the cross on the sabbath (for that sabbath was a high day), they asked Pilate that their legs might be broken, and that they might be taken away. So the soldiers came and broke the legs of the first, and of the other who had been crucified with him; but when they came to Jesus and saw that he was already dead, they did not break his legs. But one of the soldiers pierced his side with a spear, and at once there came out blood and water. He who saw it has borne witness—his testimony is true, and he knows that he tells the truth—that you also may believe. For these things took place that the scripture might be fulfilled, "Not a bone of him shall be broken." And again another scripture says, "They shall look on him whom they have pierced."
>
> After this Joseph of Arimathea, who was a disciple of Jesus, but secretly out of fear, asked Pilate that he might take away the body of Jesus, and Pilate gave him leave. So he came and took away his body. Nicodemus also, who had at first come to Jesus by night, came

bringing a mixture of myrrh and aloes about a hundred pounds' weight. They took the body of Jesus, and bound it in linen cloths with the spices, as is the burial custom of the Jews. Now in the place where he was crucified there was a garden, and in the garden a new tomb where no one had ever been laid. So because of the Jewish day of Preparation, as the tomb was close at hand, they laid Jesus there.

John 19:31-42

Ever since we lived in Santa Barbara from the mid-seventies through the mid-eighties, I have thought about Holy Saturday as the day of the earth. One of my mentors in religious studies at the university would hold a day of reflection at a retreat center in the foothills just outside the city. The setting was beautiful, nestled in a throng of oak trees, with a stunning view of the low hills with their shrubbery in shades of olive, purple, and brown and the outskirts of the city below that ended in the haze of the distant seashore.

The subject of the Saturday retreat varied slightly from year to year but basically we celebrated the quiet and hiddenness of the entombment. We acknowledged the stunned, uncomprehending grief of the disciples who no doubt could not find easy words for what they had undergone. And we experienced, in the peace-filled beauty of that place, the divine power present in creation.

The early fathers of the church understood well that the Christ event was of cosmic significance, that creation itself, more assuredly than individual souls, was transformed by the redemptive dynamic of God-with-us. A transfiguring energy entered the world in God's joining divinity to humanity and raising humanity to deified life. This cosmic perspective pervades the sensibilities of Eastern Orthodox Christianity. Salvation is envisioned not primarily as the rescue of the individual sinner through the sacrifice on the cross but as the transfiguration of the entire world through the descending-ascending process of God becoming what we are and our becoming what God is.[29] The whole created order participates in this transformation.

Clement of Alexandria, a late second-century theologian and apologist for the Christian religion during its formative years, articulated this patristic emphasis on the Christ event as significant for all creation.

Where he came from and who he was, he showed by what he taught and by the evidence of his life. He showed that he was the herald, the reconciler, our saviour, the Word, a spring of life and peace flooding over the whole face of the earth. Through him . . . the universe has already become an ocean of blessings.[30]

Likewise, Athanasius, fourth-century bishop of Alexandria and prime architect of the doctrinal formulations that became normative in the tradition, reiterated Clement's sentiments. For them both, as for the Eastern Orthodox tradition which draws heavily upon the Greek apologists, the entire creation is embraced in the deep creatureward descent of divine love in the person of Christ, whom Athanasius personified as Wisdom.

> Like a musician who has attuned his lyre, and by the artistic blending of low and high and medium tones produces a single melody, so the Wisdom of God, holding the universe like a lyre, adapting things heavenly to things earthly, and earthly things to heavenly, harmonizes them all, and, leading them by his will, makes one world and one world-order in beauty and harmony.[31]

Descent into the Depths

Clearly for these Greek-speaking Christians our human reconciliation with God was effected by the entire dynamic of the Christ-coming. The salvific emphasis was placed upon the incarnation as much as upon the crucifixion. And the sense of redemption was universal and creation-centered rather than individual and focused solely upon humankind. This is a precious insight to take forward with us into the twenty-first century as we grow increasingly aware of the symbiotic and endangered relationship between our own species and all the species in the ecosystems of the earth. God is not simply above the earth, raising us up from our God-lessness by bypassing the created order. Rather, God in Christ breaks the chains that enslave us and our earth-home, and radically frees creation to realize its own intrinsic God-likeness.

The tenet of the Christian creed that declares this marvelous creation-affirming truth is found in the central section of the Apostles' Creed.

> We believe in Jesus Christ, his only Son, our Lord.
> He was conceived by the power of the Holy Spirit and born of the Virgin Mary.

He suffered under Pontius Pilate, was crucified, died and
was buried.
He descended to the dead.

This descent to the dead, an article of this ancient and now
normative Christian credo, while not deeply explored in any other quarter
of Christendom than Eastern Orthodoxy, is wonderfully rich in its
implications. The descent to the dead as it is elucidated in that tradition
speaks symbolically to the length and breadth of divine compassion, to the
extent of the redemptive promise and to the utter intimacy of a God
whose love penetrates to the furthest reaches of creation's fallen depths.

Each feast in the Orthodox world has its particular icon. The Easter
(or Pascha) icon is entitled "The Descent into Hell." The icon of the
Eastern Orthodox church is not simply a religious picture. It is both a
medium of revelation and a channel of grace. Through it, the Word of
God is expressed in form, color, and light. An icon is a window allowing a
communion between the divine archetype imaged in the icon and the
believer. In the icon, heaven and earth meet. Unlike Western art, which
portrays the Resurrection by showing Christ rising victorious from the
tomb or which elevates an empty cross, the Pascha icon envisions Christ
descending into the depths of the earth. Thus Christ is seen to enter so
profoundly into the human condition and into creation itself, that he
penetrates the deepest realm of sin and death. The icon proclaims the
breathtaking truth that by descending to the uttermost depths of fallen
creation, Christ bursts asunder the chains that hold it enslaved. Death,
corruption, sin, and evil, all the powers of darkness, are shattered by the
penetration of light.

The icon of the descent into hell shows a vigorous Christ astride the
fallen cross whose horizontal beams have cleft apart the earth. Visible in
the bowels of earth are the enchained mass of the damned who look
upward toward their redeemer. Christ, surrounded by the saints, reaches
forward and grasps the arm of a person arising out of the grave.

The Orthodox church proclaims, "Christ has risen from the dead,
by trampling down death by death, and on those in the tombs has
bestowed life." It displays the icon of the descent on the banner that sways
at the head of the liturgical procession on Pascha.

The entire Christian church affirms this deep descent to the dead in
the Apostles' Creed. But its meaning has been variously interpreted and,

with a few exceptions, rather overlooked in contemporary western theology.[32] If considered, it seems to focus on the fate of unbaptized pre-Christian pagans who await redemption in some underworld. Yet the image has much richer implications, as the Orthodox tradition suggests. Divine power is seen to permeate the farthest reaches of creation, to stretch out and offer life to the dead, to extend to the valley of the damned where the human imagination can scarcely envision divine presence. The icon powerfully proclaims: There is no place God is not.

This Is the Night

The ancient Christian communities commonly held nocturnal prayer services. These services or vigils were especially associated with the feasts of Easter and Pentecost as well as with Sunday eves and martyrs feasts. The Easter vigil remains a common feature of the Eastern Orthodox and Roman Catholic liturgical year. Sometimes observed in the middle of the night, sometimes earlier in the evening after nightfall, the vigil service is the culmination of the entire church year. As such, it draws together the whole of the Christian story and the whole of the hope to which we are heir. The vigil occurs in the darkness of night. It finds us in our own darkness, anticipating the coming light yet not able to see, not fully awake to the mystery on whose threshold we hesitate.

We begin the vigil in the depths of night as we have since the beginnings of the church. The sanctuary is swallowed in darkness. All wait in the pregnant silence. Then the paschal candle is lit and the celebrant proclaims "Christ our light." From that one candle is ignited each of the small candles those in the congregation hold. The shadowy church is gradually illuminated by the light from hundreds of flickering tapers. The radiance of the dawning resurrection light transfigures the night. The celebrant sings:

> *Rejoice, heavenly powers!*
> *Sing, choirs of angels!*
> *Exult, all creation around God's throne!*
> *Jesus Christ, our King, is risen!*
> *Sound the trumpet of salvation!*
>
> *Rejoice, O earth, in shining splendor,*
>   *radiant in the brightness of your King!*

Christ has conquered!
Glory fills you!
Darkness vanishes for ever!

Rejoice, O Mother Church!
Exult in glory!
The risen Savior shines upon you!
Let this place resound with joy,
    echoing the mighty song of all God's people! . . .

It is truly right that with full hearts and minds and voices we
    should praise the unseen God, the all-powerful Father, and
    his only Son,
Our Lord Jesus Christ.
For Christ has ransomed us with his blood, and paid for us the
    price of Adam's sin to our eternal Father!

This is our passover feast, when Christ, the true Lamb, is slain,
    whose blood consecrates the homes of all believers.

This is the night when first you saved our [forebears]:
You freed the people of Israel from their slavery and led them
    dry-shod through the sea. . . .
This is the night when Christians everywhere, washed clean of
    sin and freed from all defilement, are restored to grace and
    grow together in holiness.

This is the night when Jesus Christ broke the chains of death
    and rose triumphant from the grave. . . .

Father, how wonderful your care for us!
How boundless your merciful love!
To ransom a slave you gave away your Son.

O happy fault, O necessary sin of Adam, which gained for us so
    great a Redeemer!
Most blessed of all nights, chosen by God to see Christ rising
    from the dead!

Of this night scripture says: "The night will be clear as day: it
    will become my light, my joy."
The power of this holy night dispels all evil, washes guilt away,

restores lost innocence, brings mourners joy; it casts out
hatred, brings us peace, and humbles earthly pride.

Night truly blessed when heaven is wedded to earth and
[we are] reconciled with God!
Therefore, heavenly Father, in the joy of this night, receive our
evening sacrifice of praise, your Church's solemn offering.

Accept this Easter candle, a flame divided but undimmed, a
pillar of fire that glows to the honor of God.
Let it mingle with the lights of heaven and continue bravely
burning to dispel the darkness of this night!

May the Morning Star which never sets find this flame still
burning: Christ, that Morning Star, who came back from
the dead, and shed his peaceful light on all [humankind],
your Son who lives and reigns for ever and ever. Amen.

The scripture readings for the vigil locate us at the dawn of creation as God fashions day and night, waters and land, flying and crawling things. We are invited to remember our own story, to recall our creation, to know again God's saving actions in history: how Abraham was joined in covenant, how God led the people out of bondage in Egypt, how God foretold the final fulfillment of the covenantal promise through the prophets. We are led through the story of our salvation to the brink of the resurrection itself, the culmination of God's saving action in human history. We become a people of memory, entering once again into the astonishing truths of the past that illuminate our present reality.

We become too a gathered community, calling upon the holy men and women of years past in the litany of the saints. We continue as well the custom of baptizing catechumens and enfolding them as members of the community on this night. All who live and have lived in the faith of the church are drawn together in the liturgy, into that sacred time which transcends historic time and mantles our story with God's own story.

It is the Vigil of Easter. We gather as the people of God, mindful of our story, longing to be liberated, trusting in the promise of the dawning light. Earth itself celebrates with us. Clearly pregnant with new life, she aches to burst forth in spring. All in creation, all in our individual and communal experience that is frozen, barren, or lifeless is stirred. All that is in shadow longs for light. Hope, long dormant in our hearts, is alive. We lean into the rising, the thaw, the bursting, and the blossoming. We are young and green with the fragile, fresh scent of the new. The words of the traditional French carol, heart-rending in their sweetness, sing our hope.

Now the green blade riseth from the buried grain,
Wheat that in dark earth many days has lain;
Love lives again, that with the dead has been:
Love is come again, Like wheat that springeth green.

In the grave they laid him, Love whom men had slain,
Thinking that never he would never again,
Laid in the earth like grain that sleeps unseen;
Love is come again, Like wheat that springeth green.

Forth he came at Easter, like the risen grain,
He that for three days in the grave had lain;
Quick from the dead, my risen Lord is seen.
Love is come again, Like wheat that springeth green.

When our hearts are wintry, grieving, or in pain,
Thy touch can call us back to life again,
Fields of our hearts that dead and bare have been.
Love is come again, Like wheat that springeth green.[33]

EASTER

Break the box and shed the nard;
Stop not now to count the cost;
Hither bring pearl, opal, sard;
Reck not what the poor have lost;
Upon Christ throw all away:
Know ye, this is Easter Day.

Build His church and deck His shrine,
Empty though it be on earth;
Ye have kept your choicest wine—
Let it flow for heavenlymirth;
Pluck the harp and breathe the horn:
Know ye not 'tis Easter morn?

Gather gladness from the skies;
Take a lesson from the ground;
Flowers do ope their heavenward eyes
And a Spring-time joy have found;
Earth throws Winter's robes away,
Decks herself for Easter Day.

Beauty now for ashes wear,
Perfumes for the garb of woe,
Chaplets for dishevelled hair,
Dances for sad footsteps slow;
Open wide your hearts that they
Let in joy this Easter Day.

Seek God's house in happy throng;
Crowded let His table be;
Mingle praises, prayer, and song,
Singing to the Trinity.
Henceforth let your souls alway
Make each morn an Easter Day.

GERARD MANLEY HOPKINS
"Easter"[34]

This Is the Day

This is the day the Lord has made,
let us rejoice and be glad!

Psalm 117:24

I have always imagined it to be a chill, fog-shrouded morning. I have seen the breaking dawn spread fingers of cool light across the low backs of the tombs. I envision a place where words are swallowed by grief, where memories of past desire and exaltation lay buried in the desolate soil. Sorrow lives here. And despair.

His friends came here bearing the one whose words had ignited the wild fires of their hope. They delivered to the grave the one whose touch had made them whole. They buried their love. Now only the women remain. The rest of the followers have fled or drifted away. But the women come, repeating the ageless female motions. They come to anoint, to tend, to care for the dead. They come expecting death and find, instead, life.

> On the first day of the week, at early dawn, they went to the tomb, taking the spices which they had prepared. They found the stone rolled away from the tomb, but when they went in they did not find the body. While they were perplexed about this, behold, two people stood by them in dazzling apparel; and as they were frightened and bowed their faces to the ground, the two said to them, "Why do you seek the living among the dead? Remember how he told you, while he was still in Galilee, that the Anointed One must be delivered into the hands of sinners, and be crucified, and on the third day rise." And they remembered Jesus' words, and returning from the tomb they told all this to the eleven and to all the rest. Now it was Mary Magdalene and Joanna and Mary the mother of James and the other women with them who told this to the apostles; but these words seemed to them an idle tale, and they did not believe them.
>
> Luke 24: 1-12

The four Gospels provide us with variant accounts of the events on that first Easter morning. But all of them concur that it was the women who remained with Jesus to the end and who were first privy to the wonder of the empty tomb. Luke's version highlights the significance of this fact within the cultural context of the time. He portrays the women as messengers who were easily dismissed as telling an idle tale. They were so regarded not simply because their story was so unbelievable but because they were women. In the Jewish culture of the time a woman's witness was not deemed admissible evidence in a court of law. Women were also not to be counted as individuals in the *minyan,* the obligatory ten persons necessary to begin prayer. While women were favorably regarded in their roles as wives and mothers, Judaism of that day had little place for women such as the women who followed Jesus, women who sat at the feet of their master and learned the ways of God, women who traveled and would consider themselves proclaimers of the good news.

So it is especially striking that at the core of our faith, in the accounts that point to Resurrection itself, it is the women who are present. It is not specifically their gender that is significant as much as their marginality to positions of power and privilege. Women, like the tax collectors, sinners, like the blind, the lame, and the leper were the outsiders of the day. And all of them were singled out by Jesus during his ministry. They are here shown to be the privileged bearers of the message of the new life of Easter.

The women show us the many faces of our response to the Easter mystery. The Marcan Chronicle records three of them (Mary Magdalene, Mary the mother of James, and Salome) as being "amazed" at the apparition of a white-robed person who informs them that Jesus had risen. It proceeds to show them fleeing from the tomb, trembling and afraid. The Matthean narrative has Mary Magdalene and the "other Mary" departing from the tomb with "fear and great joy."

Of all the mysteries our faith invites us to contemplate, the Resurrection is by far the most astonishing. Not simply in the sense of being difficult to believe in a logical fashion. That, in a way, is the very point of it. The very idea of resurrection shatters all the categories of comprehension with which we make sense of our world. It draws us instead into a reality that transcends present possibility. For myself, the wonder of the Resurrection is not so much discovered in my shoulder-shrugging acknowledgement of the power of God to effect the impossible. It is discovered instead in our own capability, pried open by the sight of the empty tomb, to live into our most poignant longings, to dream our farthest dreams, and to hope with the full expansion of our hearts. We are met, at the far limits of our resources, with limitlessness. We are met at the gates of death with a freshness and fullness of life barely grasped by the wildest stretches of our imaginings.

It is said of Brother Lawrence, a seventeenth-century monastic whose little book *The Practice of the Presence of God* is something of a spiritual classic, that

> in the winter, seeing a tree stripped of its leaves, and considering that within a little time the leaves would be renewed, and after that the flowers and fruit appear, he received a high view of the providence and power of God, which has never since been effaced from his soul.[35]

So too our peering into the empty tomb forever changes us. How inexhaustibly rich the Easter event is! What astonishing proclamations we make. Death is vanquished! Sin is overcome! Creation itself becomes a font of blessings! A new covenant is trothed! For a day we live liturgically into the truths that we glimpsed off and on during the Lenten season. God's reign of justice and peace becomes ours. Mercy overflows. Wounds are healed. Love, tender and limitless and astonishing, embraces us. It is the custom of the Christian community in Tanzania at the close of the vigil to dance until the coming of the Easter dawn. What better way to celebrate the feast of feasts: to dance for sheer joy!

He Is Risen!

On Easter morning, like the spring garden that has thrown off its blanket of snow, we don our petalled, pastel apparel. Crocus, lilacs, tulips, and daffodils scent the air and adorn the fabrics of our dresses. We come washed and brushed with special care, with hats, ties, white gloves, and patent leather shoes. There are new suits and corsages, little boys in white pants and little girls in straw bonnets. We press with excitement into our pews.

The sanctuary of the church has bloomed in lilies, their white, petalled trumpets raised in concert with the trumpets of the brass choir.

> *Jesus Christ is risen today,*
> *Alleluia!*
> *Our triumphant holy day,*
> *Alleluia!*

Who did once upon the cross,
Alleluia!
Suffer to redeem our loss.
Alleluia!

Hymns of praise then let us sing,
Alleluia!
Unto Christ our heav'nly King,
Alleluia!
Who endured the cross and grave,
Alleluia!
Sinners to redeem and save.
Alleluia!

But the pains which he endured,
Alleluia!
Our salvation have procured,
Alleluia!
Now above the sky he's King,
Alleluia!
Where the angels ever sing.
Alleluia!

Sing we to our God above,
Alleluia!
Praise eternal as his love;
Alleluia!
Praise him, now his might confess,
Alleluia!
Father, Son and Spirit blest.
Alleluia![36]

The mood of the feast mirrors the unspeakable delight felt in the marrow of our bones when the first sun-drenched days of spring have banished the gloom of grey winter's chill. The peals of "alleluia" and "glory to God," absent from the liturgy since the beginning of Lent, echo over and over. The sheer miracle of life itself fascinates us. Birds. Eggs. Chicks. Bunnies. We celebrate the just-emergent, the bursting forth, the new.

Easter is not merely an event of long ago. It is not only the celebration of divine desire to be at one with humankind. It is not only the renewal of the cosmos. Nor is it simply our kindled hope for what is promised us. Easter is also realized when we are most fully alive and aware of all that is. A former bishop of Romania has been quoted as saying, "If we only knew the truth of it we would know that each day is Easter."[37]

Easter with Us

There have been a few times in my life when I felt as though I had come close to experiencing Easter as a present reality. I do not mean this lightly. Nor do I equate this Easter perception with all the other lovely, joyous, or heartwarming experiences I have been privileged to receive over the past years. Rather, this perception of Easter-with-us is quite unique, a perception at once heightened yet quite simple and, in a fashion, ordinary. Most recently, Easter-with-us has come to me in the form of iris.

The biopsy that had been done some time ago to diagnose the cause of the lump in my neck had come back questionable. The endrocrinologist on the case all along had suggested a variety of possible sources for the lump. It could be an accumulation of fluid or benign growth of some sort. Thyroids are tricky glands, I learned, and subject to a variety of disfunctions. But the culture had shown that the cells were odd and could not be dismissed as benign. We would have to do surgery to remove the growth and determine exactly its nature. So I was hospitalized. The diagnosis was thyroid cancer. Not the most welcome news, but I was assured that this type of cancer, if caught early, was completely treatable. Through a complex set of circumstances, I ended up having surgery twice in three days so that as much of the diseased tissue as possible could be removed. Needless to say, as feisty as I tend to be, I was laid very low for some time, especially in the several days during which the surgeries were performed. I was basically capable of the bare rudiments of functioning. I slept a great deal, ate next to nothing, and surfaced mainly to visit my family and the many friends who came to wish me well.

Because I do not tolerate many medications well, I quickly stopped taking the pain relievers administered by the nurses and, despite the fact that I was flat on my back, was utterly alert during my waking periods. There was much to reflect on: the diagnosis, the effect on my husband and children, my own future, the astonishing warmth and supportiveness of so many people—indeed, I experienced their love like a great rushing wave carrying me safely through the entire ordeal.

Springtime had been late in coming that year and had not graced us with many days of basking warmth. Storms had done away with blossoms before they had a chance to mature. Even the early crocus and daffodils had been squelched. So by the time I was hospitalized in early June, we were all aching to enjoy the sights and scents of spring. The days were still intermittently rainy and overcast but the storms not severe enough to damage the later blooming flowers. Peonies were just emerging and the iris were in full bloom. I have always found iris beautiful. There is a dramatic bank of them against the south wall of the church we attend and every year their flowering delights me. But my enjoyment has always been somewhat abstracted. Bustling into choir practice I would notice and remark on the clusters of tall purple stalks, or while out walking the dog I would smile contentedly at the varieties of iris poking their heads up around our neighborhood.

When I was hospitalized, so many people sent flowers. Formal bouquets from florists, handpicked bunches from gardens, cut flowers and potted plants lined the window sill of the hospital room, crowded the bedside tables, and adorned my bedtray. There was not a free space where flowers were not. The scent was wonderful, fresh, moist, and alive. Several of the bouquets contained iris. I am not sure I had ever really reflected on iris before, not deeply and at close range. One floral arrangement especially claimed my attention. It consisted of two stalks of iris cut from a friend's garden. Unlike the usual midnight purple or lavender, this iris was a milky brown with honey-colored accents. It was also quite small, and each stalk was crowded with buds waiting, one by one, to open out into flower.

The physical ordeal of the surgeries as well as the intense emotional experience of the diagnosis had both slowed me down and heightened my awareness of things. Mostly, I was aware of being a recipient of caretaking, of concern, of attention of all kinds. Used to being the doer, or at least the one who receives in response to having done something, I was overwhelmed with the gratuity of the gifts I was offered. And I allowed myself to receive them. Indeed, I had little choice, because doing anything was out of the question.

It was the iris that became for me the symbol of this utterly astonished receptivity that I experienced. Lying on my bed, without much range of motion possible with my neck, I was nonetheless able to watch the iris in the bouquets. Over the period of a week they slowly and graciously unfolded their gifts to me. Each day, a new tightly furled bud would begin its slow-motion self-revelation, until by the end of the day it would be in full expansion. Next morning, it would have closed in on itself only to allow the next bud positioned farther down the stalk to display its breathtaking beauty. The very being of the iris, their incomprehensible delicacy and extravagance, the furry, petaled dip and curve of them, the modulations of color, the various textures of stalk, stem, stamen, and pistil all elegantly displayed themselves for my wonderment.

There was a wordlessness to the experience that is impossible to convey. The iris simply were. They were inexpressible gifts. Unique. Unrepeatable. Unforgettable if only I could be present to really see and receive them. I knew I had never seen iris before. I was not sure I had ever really seen anything before. But now I knew. I had seen iris.

Easter, that utterly gratuitous gift, is ours. It is with us in the ordinary fabric of our lives. Like a fog-shrouded morning where death and sorrow reign until the fullness of life unfurls itself and rises with the sun. Easter is ours if only we can allow ourselves to see.

THE FIFTY DAYS OF EASTER

Rise heart; thy Lord is risen. Sing his praise
    Without delays,
Who takes thee by the hand, that thou likewise
    With him mayst rise:
That, as his death calcined thee to dust,
His life may make thee gold, and much more just.

Awake, my lute, and struggle for thy part
    With all thy art.
The cross taught all wood to resound his name,
    Who bore the same.
His stretched sinews taught all strings, what key
Is best to celebrate this most high day.

Consort both heart and lute, and twist a song
    Pleasant and long:
Or since all music is but three parts vied
    And multiplied;
Oh let thy blessed Spirit bear a part,
    And make up our defects with his sweet art.

GEORGE HERBERT
"Easter I" [38]

I Have Seen the Lord

The church celebrates Easter Day for an entire week. Easter Sunday through the Sunday following is known as the Easter Octave, and it is appropriate throughout the week to worship with the same mood of exultant celebration as one does on Easter Day. The practice of extending the festivities throughout the octave following a feast dates back to the twelfth century. During the Middle Ages numerous feasts were observed in this way. Today it is only in the Roman communion that the seminal feasts of Easter and Christmas still receive this sort of recognition.

The liturgies of the Easter Octave testify to our collective desire to linger in the atmosphere of the great mysteries of our faith. Incarnation, crucifixion, and resurrection are not truths easily plumbed and quickly exhausted. As with any beautiful or meaningful happening, it is natural to want to linger, savor, retell, and re-experience. In so doing we come to understand more clearly and appreciate more deeply what we have been given.

So we observe the Octave. Furthermore, we extend the season of Easter itself for fifty days. During this period we are given the time to admire and become familiar with the gift we opened so hastily on the festal morning. I find this liturgical lingering a marvelously countercultural undertaking. Our habit as Americans is to turn holidays into commercial transactions. Weeks before Easter, stores stock their shelves with greeting cards, straw baskets, plush bunnies, and chocolate eggs. We are lured into leaping ahead of the subdued Lenten solemnity into the colorful emblems of Eastertime. Yet as soon as Easter Day has passed, the unsold marshmallow chicks and yellow and lavender crepe paper are marked down and moved out to make room for Mothers' Day cards and gifts for the graduates. Easter is banished from our awareness as we are cajoled into planning ahead for the next round of obligatory consumption. If we had any sort of openhearted encounter with the mystery of Christ's resurrection we are certainly not encouraged by our culture to allow it to sink in and ripen in our lives. So the long, festive liturgical season of the Fifty Days is a welcome counterpoint to our culture's casual dismissal of the holy day.

During the Fifty Days the scripture readings focus our attention first on the post-Resurrection appearances of Christ. We follow the bewildered disciples, still grief-stricken and disoriented, as they slowly awake to the full comprehension of what has taken place. Then, as they receive the message of their risen Lord, they once again gather together as a community. We follow them for forty days until Christ's ascension and wait with them ten more days until the promised Spirit is poured out at Pentecost.

Simultaneous with this unfolding drama of the Fifty Days we are made privy to the continuing story of the post-Pentecost community, the early church. We read frequently from the Acts of the Apostles. We hear of the enspirited disciples going forth, baptizing, healing, and preaching, despite resistance and actual persecution. We learn of their struggles to create community, first as a small sectarian group, then as they expand beyond their Jewish origins to become a faith embraced by many peoples. The readings from the Acts of the Apostles challenge us to reflect on the nature of Christian community as the realization of the Easter event. They also encourage us to attend to the variety of ways the faithful over the centuries have embodied the hope of Easter Day.

The Gospel readings for the Fifty Days come mainly from the Book of John. This Gospel best captures the power of the risen Christ and most clearly links the mission of Jesus with the continuing work of the Holy Spirit in the community of faith. It is John which provides us with the "I am" scriptures which capture in unforgettable imagery the fullness of the risen Christ. In them he is revealed as the bread of life, the vine, and the good shepherd.

Witnesses to the Good News

There are many years during which I have felt that I wasn't quite up to Easter. Having lived into the mood of the Lenten season I might find myself fixated on Good Friday or unable to rise from the earth of Holy Saturday. Some years I feel like I haven't even "done" Lent. Despite efforts to immerse myself in the season, I remain outside the sense of it, distracted by other concerns. Even in years when the circumstances of my life coincide with my attention to the liturgical calendar and I come willing and awe-struck to the empty tomb, the very brightness and magnificence of the Easter event often seems impossible to grasp. Everything is white lilies and brass choirs and I'm not quite prepared to assimilate it. I identify with the fear-filled, distraught apostles who cannot imagine what they have been told. I need the appearance narratives to very slowly and insistently show me what has occurred.

The Johannine narrative records the first appearance as taking place just outside the tomb. Mary Magdalene, who was the first to discover that Jesus was not where they had laid him, runs to tell the news to Peter and John. They in turn search the tomb but find only an empty shroud. Mary remains alone in the garden, lost in her newly compounded grief.

> Mary stood weeping outside the tomb, and as she wept she stooped to look into the tomb; she saw two angels in white, sitting where the body of Jesus had lain, one at the head and one at the feet. They said to her, "Woman why are you weeping?" She said to them, "Because they have taken away my Lord, and I do not know where they have laid him." Saying this, she turned round and saw Jesus standing, but she did not know that it was Jesus. Jesus said to her, "Woman, why are you weeping? Whom do you seek?" Supposing him to be the gardener, she said to him, "Sir, if you have carried him away, tell me where you have laid him, and I will take him away." Jesus said to her, "Mary." She turned and said to him in Hebrew, "Rabboni!" (which means Teacher). Jesus said to her, "Do not hold me, for I have not yet ascended to the One from whom I came; but go to my other companions and say to them, I am ascending to God who is my . . . Father as God is . . . Father to you." Mary Magdalene went and said to the others, "I have seen the Lord"; and she told them that he had said these things to her.
>
> John 20:11-18

I was once at an intimate mass where this Gospel was the reading of the day (it was the Easter octave). The presider opted to allow those gathered to share their personal reflections on the scene. We were to listen prayerfully to the text and to imagine ourselves in the place of Mary Magdalene hearing our own name called. Then we were invited to share our responses. The reflections varied. The presider recalled feeling that it was too good to be true. Another worshipper identified with Mary's sense of the changed relationship: Jesus was with her but she could no longer touch him. I remember feeling overwhelmed at being recognized and met in the depth of my grief. I/Mary had lost what was dearest in life. The desolation felt in that realization was overwhelming. Yet when hope was gone, my name was called.

This dimension of the Easter event is astonishing. If only we could really hear our name called in those parts of ourselves and our world where hopelessness holds fast.

I think in this regard of the diaries of a young Jewish woman, Etty Hillesum, who died during the holocaust of World War II.[39] The diaries are a moving testimony to the power of love realized in the darkest hours of human experience. At her diary's beginning Etty was not an observant Jew, nor did she ever become ritually devout. She was a student of some intellectual promise, studying philosophy and literature. She lived a fairly bohemian life, being romantically linked with a fellow student and later with an older mentor who was involved in the burgeoning field of psychology. When Nazi forces occupied her native Holland, she had an opportunity to leave the country on a special permit but decided to stay with her fellow religionists.

What is so gripping about the diary is not the account of what happened to her (the entries break off when she is shipped off to the concentration camps, where she died). What grips the reader is the growing luminousness of her perception. She begins as a bright, thoughtful, but rather typically arrogant young woman. Gradually she begins to see the world and the events around her with breathtaking compassion. Central to her transformation is her awakening desire to become a person who can kneel. Somehow the capacity to bend in awe and adoration was for her the key to unlocking life's utter beauty and mystery. As her diary unfolds, the reader observes her meeting the growing menace and horror of Nazi oppression with the ability to see deeply into the human condition. She knows the outrage, yet she also knows the unbearable pain of both oppressor and oppressed. Her tender portrayals of broken humanity are fearless in their clarity and empathy. In the depths of hopelessness, Etty Hillesum found and became love. This young Jewish woman had heard the call of her name as Magdalene did long ago, and it transfigured her.

Throughout the Easter Octave a number of the appearance narratives from various Gospels are proclaimed in the liturgy. We hear Matthew's account of Jesus' meeting with the women who were fleeing from the empty tomb (Matt. 28:8-15). We recall Luke's story of the two disciples on the road to Emmaus who fail to recognize Jesus as the stranger on the road as well as Jesus' manifestation to the eleven gathered in Jerusalem (Luke 24:13-49). From John's Gospel we retell the tale of Jesus' revealing himself to his companions by the Sea of Tiberias (John 21:1-25). In Mark we read a synopsis of the various appearances alluded to in other parts of the Gospels (Mark 16:9-15). Over and over we are presented with the miracle of the Resurrection. Where hopelessness held sway, hope is born anew. We acknowledge one another with the traditional Orthodox greeting and response of the entire Easter season.

> Christ is risen!
> He is risen indeed!

The text recalls the "taking up" of the Old Testament prophets Enoch and Elijah from the realm of earth to that of God. Yet the ascension is different from these Hebrew precedents in that it is subsumed into the fact of the Resurrection. According to the New Testament writers, that Easter reality, which is a nonspatial transformation of death into a share of the divine glory, took place instantly "on the third day." The ascension then is a spatial image to express the reality of the final withdrawal of the risen Jesus' physical presence from the assembled disciples. The feast also marks the beginning of the church and Christ's incarnate presence now experienced in that body. The risen, cosmic Christ takes his glorified place as head of the body-church organism.

> May the God of our Lord Jesus Christ, the God of glory, give you a spirit of wisdom and of revelation in the knowledge of God, having the eyes of your hearts enlightened, that you may know what is the hope to which you have been called, what are the riches of God's glorious inheritance in the saints, and what is the immeasurable greatness of God's power in us who believe, according to the working of God's great might which was accomplished in Christ when God raised him from the dead and made him sit at the holy throne in the heavenly places, far above all rule and authority and power and dominion, and above every name that is named, not only in this age but also in that which is to come; putting all things under Christ's feet and making him the head over all things for the church, which is his body, the fullness of God who fills all in all.
>
> Ephesians 1:17-23

Lord of the Dance

The ascension is depicted in a variety of ways in western art. One of the most delightful motifs I know of was discovered by a friend. He found it painted on the ceiling of a church in England. There, in a bank of clouds, were the soles of two feet, obviously the last bit of the embodied Lord that the assembled disciples glimpsed before he left them.

Although I know of no extended theological commentary on the significance of feet in the Christian story, to my mind, feet are worthy of note. Feet are the part of the body most connected to the earth. Feet are essential in any mobility; they were the primary mode of locomotion in the ancient world. Feet feature in the biblical narrative frequently. The disciples were urged to shake the dust from their feet if they entered a city unresponsive to their message (Mark 6:11). Jesus washed the feet of his disciples (John 13:1-20). His in turn were washed by the woman at the Pharisee's house (Luke 7:36-50). Mary of Bethany sat at the feet of her teacher, Jesus, to learn the ways of God (Luke 10: 38-42). The wonderful prophecies of Isaiah, applied to Jesus, declare

> How beautiful on the mountains,
> are the feet of the messenger announcing peace,
> Of the messenger of good news,
> who proclaims salvation
> and says to Zion,
> "Your God is king!"
>
> Isaiah 52:7, NJB

The passage from Ephesians read on the feast of the Ascension places all things in creation under the feet of Christ.

I think particularly of feet when I think of the risen Christ at Easter time. For Jesus himself was the one who danced on his grave. With nimble feet, he rose up prancing, trampling death and sorrow underfoot. At Easter we are invited to do the same. All in our lives that is limiting, sorrowful, or dead becomes the dance floor on which we celebrate our Easter joy.

There have, in fact, been communities of Christians who felt it incumbent upon themselves to live and worship in the spirit of this dance. One such community, which after its inception became a religious movement distinct from Christianity, was the Shakers or the United Society of Believers in Christ's Second Appearing. The Shakers took their origin from a revival of the Quakers in England in the mid-eighteenth century and their early leadership from a charismatic woman named Ann Lee, known as Mother Ann. Moving to America after a period of persecution, the Shakers settled in upstate New York. There they established a utopian community in which all rose at a common hour, wore uniform dress, took meals together and, in the case of senior members, held property in common. A celibate community of both women and men, the Shakers practiced a spirituality of the perfected ordinary. All routine tasks, environments, or implements were to have the utmost simplicity, function, and beauty.

The Shakers' name is derived from the ecstatic shaking they exhibited while at worship, shaking which was later choreographed into a precise dance for those worshiping in common. It is to a traditional Shaker melody that the contemporary song, "Lord of the Dance" is set. Its lyrics are inspired by the imagery of that tradition's spirituality.

I danced in the morning when the world was begun,
And I danced in the moon and the stars and the sun,
And I came down from heaven and I danced on the earth;
At Bethlehem I had my birth.

(Refrain)
Dance then wherever you may be;
I am the Lord of the dance, said he,
And I'll lead you all, wherever you may be,
And I'll lead you all in the dance, said he.

I danced for the scribe and the pharisee,
But they wouldn't dance, and they wouldn't follow me;
I danced for the fishermen, for James and John;
They came with me and the dance went on.

(Refrain)

I danced on the Sabbath and I cured the lame:
The holy people said it was a shame.
They whipped and they stripped and they hung me high,
And left me there on a cross to die.

(Refrain)

I danced on a Friday when the sky turned black;
It's hard to dance with the devil on your back.
They buried my body and they thought I'd gone;
But I am the dance and I still go on.

(Refrain)

They cut me down and I leap up high;
I am the life that'll never, never die;
I'll live in you if you'll live in me:
I am the Lord of the Dance, said he.[55]

(Refrain)

At the liturgical moment of the ascension we observe the time during which the feet of Jesus last made intimate contact with the earth. This Jesus was God very much with us, feet firmly planted on the ground. Now a new relationship between God and the earth-home we inhabit begins. As Spirit, God would enter the community of believers and inspire them to take up the journey, to be the feet that bring good news, the teachers at whose feet disciples sit, the foot-washers and those whose feet are washed, the feet that dance upon the grave.

From Glory to Glory

Several days after my father died I had a dream in which he appeared. In the dream I was above the clouds, very much as one is in an airplane, and could look down and see a vast, thick pillow of cloud stretching from horizon to horizon. The light coming from the atmosphere above was so brilliant it hurt the eyes. Light shone blazing and white on the surface of the cloud cover. My father was standing on the clouds, below and facing away from me. He appeared to be about forty years old, very much the image of the man captured in photos taken the Christmas I was five: a vital man of medium height, with the flair of an artist and a sense of whimsical delight. In the dream my father wore a nightshirt and, as I watched him from behind and above, he began to dance. He leapt and jigged and cavorted. Then he began to laugh. Peals of laughter burst joyfully out of him. Free, I thought, he is free at last. I will remember him this way always, utterly himself, utterly free, dancing and laughing for sheer joy.

We enter the seventh week of Easter with a sense of anticipation for the coming of the Comforter Jesus has promised. Jesus has ascended, and we remain, as it were, gathered beneath the disappearing soles of his feet awaiting the descent of the promised Comforter. The readings of the liturgical moment emphasize the glory into which Jesus enters. They stress his identity with God the creator, the cosmic scope of divine identity, and our identity with the glory to which and from which he comes. There is vastness in this week's scriptures and a sense of the enormous height, length, and depth of the hope to which we are called.

From the Book of Revelation we read the prophetic words of John which situate Jesus at the beginning and end of time. The passage ties together creation, God's action through history, and the end times with the thread of the Jesus story.

[I, John, heard a voice saying to me:] "Behold, I am coming soon, bringing my recompense, to repay everyone for what each has done. I am the Alpha and the Omega, the first and the last, the beginning and the end."

Blessed are those who wash their robes, that they may have the right to the tree of life and that they may enter the city by the gates.

"I, Jesus, have sent my angel to you with this testimony for the churches. I am the root and the offspring of David, the bright morning star."

The Spirit and the Bride say, "Come." Let those who hear say, "Come." Let those who are thirsty, come, let those who desire take the water of life without price.

The One who testifies to these things says, "Surely I am coming soon." Amen. Come, Lord Jesus!

Revelation 22:12-14, 16-17, 20

From John's Gospel Jesus is heard to speak of his glorious identity and, through him, that self-same identity is promised to those whose identity is one in Christ:

Jesus lifted up his eyes to heaven and said, "Abba, the hour has come; glorify me that I may glorify you, since you have given me power over all flesh, to give eternal life to all whom you have given me. And this is eternal life, that they know you the only true God, and Jesus Christ whom you have sent. I glorified you on earth, having accomplished the work which you gave me to do; and now, glorify me in your own presence with the glory which I had with you before the world was made.

"I have manifested your name to those whom you gave me out of the world; yours they were, and you gave them to me, and they have kept your word. Now they know that everything that you have given me is from you; for I have given them the words which you gave me, and they have received them and know in truth that I came from you; and they have believed that you did send me. I am praying for them; I am not praying for the world but for those whom you have given me, for they are yours; all mine are yours, and yours are mine, and I am glorified in them. And now I am no more in the world, but they are in the world, and I am coming to you."

John 17:1-11

In many church circles this image of Jesus as glorified Lord is the dominant image that underpins devotion, theological reflection, and worship. I must admit that my own sense of the Christ event is more distinctly incarnational. God-with-us in the mysticism of minutia is more in tune with my spirit than the abstract glorified God-man who reigns in some distant heaven. Yet, if a quasi-Apollinarianism (the ancient heresy that asserts Jesus to be a god in the guise of mortal flesh) is avoided, the expansiveness of this week's readings can give us real insight into the full range of the Christian story.

It is so easy to think we can claim, name, and delineate God. We have revelation, we have the teachings of the church, we have a deeply inbred sense of convention that clarifies for us what God is and what God is not. This is holy, this is not, we say, walking the clearly demarcated boundaries between church and not church, sacred and secular, good and bad, clean and unclean, believer and non-believer, solemn and frivolous, worthy and unworthy.

I would suggest, with a very ancient tradition to back me up, that God is less like what we know than what we do not know, that God's ways and nature and glory are best grasped through a sense unavailable to ordinary senses and thought. This is, of course, an ancient idea in the cumulative tradition. It is found most clearly in the writings of the patristic era—the church fathers of the first several centuries—and has received elaboration in both the Eastern Orthodox tradition and the Christian west. Among the writers that affirmed the basic incomprehensibility of God in God's essence was Gregory of Nyssa, a Cappadocian Christian of the fourth century and one of the most noted theologians of his own and later times. Gregory certainly asserted that God was authentically revealed in scripture and tradition. But he also affirmed that, beyond this, God in the glory of divine essence was unknowable. The closest one could approach the essential divine was through mystical apprehension, a sort of ecstatic unknowing that was best analogically described as darkness, because the ordinary human senses and mental capacities could not grasp it. In his treatise, *The Life of Moses*, Gregory employs the biblical prophet's story to illustrate this teaching on the ultimate incomprehensibility of God.

> What now is the meaning of Moses' entry into the darkness and of the vision of God that he enjoyed in it? . . . The sacred text is here teaching us that . . . as the soul makes progress, and by a greater and more perfect concentration comes to appreciate what the knowledge of truth is, the more it approaches this vision, and so much the more does it see that the divine nature is invisible. It thus leaves all surface appearances, not only those that can be grasped by the senses but

also those which the mind itself seems to see, and it keeps on going deeper until by the operation of the spirit it penetrates the invisible and incomprehensible, and it is there that it sees God. The true vision and the true knowledge of what we seek consists precisely in not seeing, in an awareness that our goal transcends all knowledge and is everywhere cut off from us by the darkness of incomprehensibility. Thus that profound evangelist, John, who penetrated into this luminous darkness, tells us that *no man hath seen God at any time*, teaching us by this negation that no man—indeed, no created intellect—can attain a knowledge of God.[56]

This idea of the ultimate incomprehensibility of God is elicited for me by the readings of the week. They speak of ends and beginnings, alpha and omega, height and depth, glory inconceivable. They tend, in my mind, to qualify all our self-assured assertions about God and the things of God. They invite me, not to idolize what we know and say of God, but to refuse to make idols of doctrinal formulations, rites of worship, or language that points to God. While honoring tradition with its revealed basis in scripture, I am also aware of being invited to allow God to be God, and to allow myself to dance free and unfettered in joyous delight in the glory to which I am called.

The Glory You Have Given Me

Gregory of Nyssa's vision of the Christian life, in keeping with the ethos of his time, was a vision of moving from "glory" to "glory." According to him, humankind was created to be deified or made one with God. Human life was a progressive movement toward God-likeness, a concentration on and unification with the divine. This was effected in stages of spiritual growth, a sort of perpetual re-creation, a constant beginning again at ever more transformed levels of being. One never "arrived" in this process but plunged deeper and deeper into divine darkness; each "glory" or stage of the journey, when reached, gave way to the next "glory" which rose up beyond.

The Johannine readings of the Seventh Week of Easter emphasize the fact that Christ's glory is also ours and that, in Christ, we all share this one glory, this one incomprehensible divine life.

[Jesus lifted up his eyes to heaven and said:] "I do not pray for these only, but also for those who believe in me through their word, that they may all be one; even as you, O God, are in me, and I in you, that they also may be in us, so that the world may believe that you have sent me. The glory which you have given me I have given to them, that they may be one even as we are one, I in them and you in me, that they may become perfectly one, so that the world may know that you have sent me and have loved them even as you have loved me. O Holy One, I desire that they also, whom you have given me, may be with me where I am, to behold my glory which you have given me in your love for me before the foundation of the world. O righteous God, the world has not known you, but I have known you; and these know that you have sent me. I made known to them your name, and I will make it known, that the love with which you have loved me may be in them, and I in them."

John 17:20-26

It is so easy for us to say that the divine glory we share with the God who is love is manifested in love. How difficult it is, however, to realize! And yet all of us know from experience that the manifestation of genuine love between individuals or communities of all sorts is clearly experienced as the presence of God.

One community of Christians that seeks to realize this profound love is the ecumenical community of Taizé. Taizé is a tiny village hidden in the south of France in the hills of Burgundy which, since 1940, has been the home of an ecumenical community of men who observe the ancient practice of daily liturgical prayer in common. To this community flock tens of thousands of visitors yearly, all of whom come to pray and worship together. Taizé began as the dream of a young Frenchman whose consciousness of the need for human reconciliation was shaped by the horrors of World War II. Brother Roger, the group's founder, had given refuge to Jews fleeing the Nazi occupation. After the war he retired to a life of solitude to listen to the whisper of God's voice. Soon he was joined by other men, mostly Protestant Christians, who vowed themselves to celibacy and dedicated themselves to the purposes of reconciliation. Eventually, joined by Roman Catholic brethren, the community became international in character. The brothers presently come from some twenty different countries throughout the world. Gradually, a worldwide apostolate developed, and today small groups of brothers live among the poor on different continents or travel in small bands. From its beginning Taizé has focused on reconciliation among Christian denominations. This particular reconciliation has not been an end in itself. Reconciliation among all humanity is Taizé's dream, the church being the first place of communion for all.

Taizé has been especially popular among young people from many different countries who have made massive pilgrimages to the hills of Burgundy to share the prayers of the community and their lives and concerns with one another. The first such "Council of Youth," held in 1970 attracted forty thousand participants. This ecumenical community with love large enough to embrace the entire human race is an outstanding example of the scriptural vision of ultimate glory envisioned in the gospel of this Easter seventh week. It enfleshes the text of the ninth century Latin hymn, *Ubi Cáritas*, so familiar to us even today.

> *(Refrain)*
> *Where true love and charity are found,*
> *God is always there.*
>
> *Since the love of Christ has brought us all together,*
> *Let us all rejoice and be glad, now and always.*
> *Let everyone love the Lord God, the living God;*
> *And with sincere hearts let us love each other now.*
>
> *Therefore when we gather as one in Christ Jesus,*
> *Let our love enfold each race, creed, ev'ry person,*
> *Let envy, division and strife cease among us;*
> *May Christ our Lord dwell among us in every heart.*
>
> *Bring us with your saints to behold your great beauty,*
> *There to see you, Christ our God, throned in great glory;*
> *There to possess heaven's peace and joy, your truth and love,*
> *For endless ages of ages, world without end.*[57]

PENTECOST

We Believe in the one High God,
Who out of love created the beautiful world and
    everything good in it.
Who created people and wanted them to be happy
    in the world.
God loves the world
And every nation and tribe on the earth.
We have known this High God in the darkness,
And now we know God in the light.
God promised in the Book of the Word,
The Bible,
to save the world and all nations and tribes.

We Believe that God
Made good this promise, by sending a son,
Jesus Christ,
A man in the flesh,
A Jew by tribe,
Born poor in a little village,
Who left His home, and was always on safari
    doing good,
Curing people by the power of God,
Teaching them about God
    and humanity.   .

Showing that the meaning of religion
Is love.
He was rejected by His people,
Tortured and nailed, hands and feet to a cross
And died.
He lay buried in the grave,
But the hyenas did not touch Him,
And on the third day He rose from the grave.
He ascended to the skies.
He is the Lord.

We Believe that all our sins are forgiven
    through Him.
All who have faith in Him, must be sorry for
    their sins,
Be baptized in the Holy Spirit of God,
Live the rules of love,
And share the bread together, in love,
To announce the Good News to others, until
    Jesus comes again.
We are waiting for Him.
He is alive.
He lives.
This we believe. Amen.

THE CREED OF THE MASAI PEOPLE[58]

To Drink of One Spirit

It is the eve of Pentecost, the celebration of the coming of the promised Spirit. It is the vigil of the day that commemorates the beginning of the church as bearer of the divine breath. Through the Word the church recalls several dramatic instances in the life of the covenant community. We read of the descent of the Most High to the mountain of Sinai, coming amidst peals of thunder and fire to give Moses the Law (Exod. 19:3-8, 16-20). We read how God claimed the prophet Ezekiel and sent him into a valley of death to breathe life into and put flesh upon dry bones (Ezek. 37:1-14). We read of the tower of Babel, of the scattering and confusion of the earth's people who, suddenly many-tongued, can no longer understand one another (Gen. 11:1-9).

On the eve of Pentecost we read these tales of divine initiative in history. We are given images from the Old Testament that prepare us for the enspiriting event on whose threshold we hover. Like the descent of God to give the law on Sinai, the descent of the Spirit will provide God's people with a path, a way. But this new way will come not from without but from within, from the dynamic movement of the divine presence activating the minds and hearts of the people. In the manner of the prophet Ezekiel, the coming Spirit will breathe vibrant life into all that is dry and lifeless. The Spirit of God will enter into the dry bones of our individual and communal graves and animate us with divine dynamism. To reverse the babbling of the scattered, confused nations, God will send one Spirit to allow us to speak in tongues so that all may comprehend. God will unify the people. God will grant gifts so that all might be gifted, one through the other. God will slake the thirst of all who desire to drink the living water. And all shall drink of one Spirit.

In years gone by the liturgical mood of Pentecost was one of great pageantry and beauty. The eye was greeted with brilliant red banners and vestments. The sense of smell caught the rising clouds of incense as they purified the holy space of the sanctuary. The ear was delighted with the musical setting of the ninth century hymn *Veni, Creator Spiritus,* or perhaps with its nineteenth-century translation:

Come Holy Ghost, Creator blest,
And in our hearts take up thy rest;
Come with thy grace and heav'nly aid
To fill the hearts which thou hast made,
To fill the hearts which thou hast made.

O Comforter, to thee we cry,
Thou heav'nly gift of God most high;
Thou fount of life, and fire of love,
And sweet anointing from above,
And sweet anointing from above.

O Holy Ghost, through thee alone,
Know we the Father and Son;
Be this our firm, unchanging creed,
That thou dost from them both proceed,
That thou dost from them both proceed.

Praise we the Lord, Father and Son,
And Holy Spirit with them one;
And may the Son on us bestow
All gifts that from the Spirit flow,
All gifts that from the Spirit flow.[59]

In years past the church celebrated the feast of Pentecost, or Whitsunday as it is known in the Church of England, with almost as much solemnity as Easter. Historically, it ranks second only to the feast of the Resurrection. The feast merited a vigil on the evening before and an octave during the week following. For whatever reason, we seem to have lost track of this day as one of special celebration. It certainly never attracts the same crowds as Christmas or Easter Day. Despite this, the day is one of great significance. It culminates the cycle of Lent and Easter. It comes full circle in the dynamic movement of the dying and rising we experience during that season.

Prophetic Community

The term *Pentecost* was the Greek name given to the Jewish agricultural Feast of Weeks which fell on the fiftieth day after Passover (Pentecost means "the fiftieth day"). According to the Book of Acts this was the day on which the Holy Spirit descended upon the disciples.

When the day of Pentecost had come, they were all together in one place. And suddenly a sound came from heaven like the rush of a mighty wind, and it filled all the house where they were sitting. There appeared to them tongues as of fire, distributed and resting on each one of them. And they were all filled with the Holy Spirit and began to speak in other tongues, as the Spirit gave them utterance.

Now there were dwelling in Jerusalem Jews, devout people from every nation under heaven. At this sound the multitude came together, and they were bewildered, because all present heard them speaking in their own language. They were amazed and wondered saying, "Are not all these who are speaking Galileans? And how is it we hear, each of us in our own native language? Parthians and Medes and Elamites and residents of Mesopotamia, Judea and Cappadocia, Pontus and Asia, Phrygia and Pamphylia, Egypt and the parts of Libya belonging to Cyrene, and visitors from Rome, both Jews and proselytes, Cretans and Arabians, we hear them telling in our own tongues the mighty works of God."

Acts 2:1-11

This text from the Acts of the Apostles is theologically rich. The particular allusions in this account (there are two other references to Pentecost in the New Testament, later in Acts 20:16 and in 1 Corinthians 16:8) link the event with the giving of the law to Moses at Mount Sinai (Exod. 19-20). The reconstituted disciples are gathered like the twelve tribes at Sinai. The sound from heaven, the filling of the *whole* house (like the shaking of the whole mountain), and the fire recall the theophany at Sinai.

During the formative era of the church the Feast of Weeks was in fact associated with the giving of the Law, just as the agricultural festival of Unleavened Bread or Passover was associated with the Israelites' deliverance out of Egypt. So it was natural for the early Christian community to see the scenario of Pentecost as a new, significant prophetic moment in God's dealing with humankind. On the feast of the giving of the Law (the privileged communication of God's word) comes the end time gift of the Holy Spirit to vitalize the new expression of the divine word through the ministry of the apostles. The list of Jewish pilgrims from various nations suggests that this is the fulfillment of the endtime gathering of Israel. The gifts of Pentecost are destined for Jews first but then will be spread to the ends of the earth.

The account of the gift of various tongues is often seen as a reversal of the story of the tower of Babel found in Genesis 11:1-9. In that narrative a sinful people are scattered in confusion and lose their ability to communicate. Here in Acts 2 a people of many languages is gathered, receives a new ability to communicate in the Spirit, and is enabled to become a community that repents of its sin and tells of the mighty works of God.

So this is a moment of prophetic significance. It marks the beginning of the church (some congregations today in fact celebrate the day that way—as a birthday—rather as Americans celebrate the Fourth of July). It affirms that the church is an enspirited continuance of the prophetic mission and power of Jesus the Christ.

The idea of the church as prophetic community has had many variations over its long history and wide denominational span. The presence of the Spirit is understood to manifest itself in dreams, inspirations, visions and prophetic pronouncements. Often the Spirit's manifestation has apocalyptic significance. It foretells the endtimes when all shall pass away. The ancient prophecy of Joel becomes the proof text for this belief.

> [Thus says the Most High:]
> "I will pour out my spirit on all flesh;
> your sons and your daughters shall prophesy,
>   the old shall dream dreams,
>   and the young shall see visions.
> Even upon the maidservants and menservants
>   in those days, I will pour out my spirit.
> "And I will give portents in the heavens and on the earth, blood and fire and columns of smoke. The sun shall be turned to darkness, and the moon to blood, before the great and terrible day of the Holy comes. And it shall come to pass that all who call upon the name of the Holy One shall be delivered; for in Mount Zion and in Jerusalem there shall be those who escape, as the Most High God has said, and among the survivors shall be those whom God has called.
>
> Joel 2:28-30

This Old Testament prophecy is directly alluded to in the second-century North African passion narrative entitled "The Martyrdoms of Sts. Perpetua and Felicitas." This extraordinary document, which preserves for us the account of the deaths of two Christian women, provides us with much insight about the self-understanding of the early church in North Africa during a period of persecution. Perpetua, a young Roman matron with a nursing baby, and a pregnant slave woman, Felicitas, are among a band of believers who seek baptism in the Christian faith. To do so is to become an enemy of Rome subject to arrest and death if faith is not recanted. Despite the entreaties of family, the two are so convinced by the promises of Christ that they willingly give up their lives. By participating with him in his death they believe they will participate in the resurrection energy that triumphs over death.

The passion narrative of these two women shows us a Christian community that knows itself as filled by the Spirit and ushered into a prophetic role in the world. First of all, the heroines of this narrative are unlikely heros for their time in history. The Greco-Roman world of their day did not admit the leadership of women or slaves. They were the disempowered of society. Yet here they were, equals in a band of martyrs that included men and free-born citizens. To the world of their time, the witness of these women spoke of the radical, prophetic nature of the Christian good news: no more are we to be seen as Gentile or Jew, slave or free, woman or man; all are one in Christ. Secondly, their witness also spoke to a culture that saw women as the embodiment of all that is biologically and socially predetermined. Such women, embracing a reality more compelling than the one that tied them to husbands, children, kin, or even the preservation of bodily life, were a startling countercultural witness to the transcendent dynamic they claimed had entered the world in Christ. Third, these heroic witnesses received dreams and visions and the various gifts of the Spirit; the capacity to reconcile, to heal, and to prophesy. Recalling the words of Joel, the redactor of the Passion narrative is convinced that the dreams and visions that these women received were signs of the outpouring of the Spirit promised at the last times.

In fact, second-century North African Christianity believed that the end time was at hand, just as the early Pauline churches did. The gifts of the Spirit were seen as manifestations of that reality. Few mainline denominations today work out of such an apocalyptic theology. We have long accommodated ourselves to not knowing the *when* of the last days. But the concept that the Spirit continues to pour out and manifest itself as prophetic community is still very much with us today.

I think in this regard of the Sojourners community in Washington, D.C., the evangelical Christian community that takes seriously the idea that the church is called to be a prophetic, countercultural witness in the world. The Sojourners group is an egalitarian, ecumenical community of persons that seeks to serve the needs of the poor in its neighborhood. It publishes a national magazine that promotes ideals of nonviolence, social justice, and biblical conversion. For the Sojourners community, the life of discipleship has political ramifications, and the group has spawned many long-range projects: for example, the ecumenical Witness for Peace in Central America. Jim Wallis, the group's spokesman, stands as a towering, prophetic figure in the wider church community, calling people to conscientious reflection on the serious social issues of our time and asking people to respond in action to their consciences as honed by a radical reading of the Bible.

Communities like Sojourners witness to the movement of the Spirit in the world, the Spirit which groans in us as it responds to the misery, the hatred, the hunger, and the despair that burdens humankind. Centuries ago Paul wrote to the church in Rome about the groaning and the indwelling of this Spirit. His words still ring true for us today:

> We know that the whole creation has been groaning in travail together until now; and not only the creation, but we ourselves, who have the first fruits of the Spirit, groan inwardly as we wait for adoption as children, the redemption of our bodies. For in this hope we were saved. Now hope that is seen is not hope. For who hopes for what they see? But if we hope for what we do not see, we wait for it with patience.
>
> Likewise, the Spirit helps us in our weakness; for we do not know how to pray as we ought, but God's own Spirit intercedes for us with sighs too deep for words. And God who searches the hearts of all knows what is the mind of the Spirit, because the Spirit intercedes for the saints according to the will of God.
>
> Romans 8:22-27

Pentecost celebrates the indwelling of God's own hope in us, incarnate in our world through our lives.

Gifts of the Spirit

One of the five mosaics that decorate the great interior domes of the Basilica of Saint Mark in Venice depicts the Pentecost event. Executed in the mid-twelfth century, the mosaic in the dome above the nave shows the twelve apostles arranged in a circle at the edge of the dome above a bank of windows. In the center of the dome is a throne, on which stands the dove of the Holy Spirit. From the throne, rays extend to each of the apostles. Below the apostles and between the windows are situated people from all nations. The Byzantine design creates a wheel-like effect overhead. From the wheel's center the empowering activity of the Spirit radiates outward to the apostles and through them to the entire world.

At Pentecost the Spirit came to empower the church as prophetic community. To accomplish this, the gifts of the Spirit were distributed to each member so that through their sharing the sum of the gifts might be available to all. The way in which this gift-giving occurred is described in the scriptures as tongues of fire riding on the wind and coming to rest on the apostles. The power and vitality of the image is captivating. The rush of wind and flame, the startled surprise of the ones being gifted, the surge of empowerment that bursts in only to burst through and extend beyond. The coming of the gifts of the Spirit is dynamic and dramatic.

Medieval tradition named the Spirit's gifts as sevenfold. They are: wisdom, understanding, counsel, fortitude, knowledge, piety, and fear of the Lord. The list was developed from the Latin (Vulgate) version of the second verse of Isaiah, chapter eleven. But in wider practice the gifts of the Spirit refer to those talents and capacities, some quite ordinary, others extraordinary, that the members of the church bring to their communal ministry and life together. In some circles the gifts of the Spirit refer to unusual charismatic talents—the gift of healing, the gift of speaking in tongues, or the gift of prophecy.

However one defines the gifts of the Spirit, one truth remains: the gifts are not given for individual enrichment or enhancement; they are given to be shared. They are meant to give life to the whole community. This is a very different way of looking at gifts than the way our culture generally does. Our talents and capacities are viewed primarily as personal possessions to be expressed in the service of our own authenticity or for our own personal advancement. There are certainly people who share their gifts, very generously, but my sense is that we usually see this as an act of self-sacrifice or of civic-mindedness; as good things that good people give from their own storehouses from altruistic motives. Rarely do we consider that the gifts were given to us precisely that they might spill out to others or that others' gifts were given that they might spill over to us. But that, in fact, is the underlying meaning of the tongues of flame riding on the wind. The domed mosaic of Saint Mark's images it well. The source of the gifts is one. They proceed outward to the apostles only to flow through them to the surrounding peoples and nations of the earth.

The early Christian church took the charismatic nature of the community seriously. And in its earliest years it apparently allowed the theology of the gift to be reflected in its patterns of ministry. Some were gifted as preachers, some as teachers, some as healers, some in other ways. The gift, no matter who offered it, was welcomed as destined for the good of the whole. As more fixed patterns of ministry developed in the formative second and third centuries, some of this sense of the charismatic nature of church leadership was lost. Women, particularly, who were active in a variety of ways—visionaries like Perpetua and Felicitas or conveners of house churches or itinerant ministers of the good news—soon found little acceptance of their gifts within the developing structure of community. This trend, of course, has been challenged over the centuries and is at the forefront of issues in many Christian churches today.

But the fact remains that the Pentecost event is at the core of our identity as church. As Jesus promised, the Spirit was sent. And it empowered the church with a variety of gifts meant to be shared. The apostle Paul said it well in his letter to the Corinthian church:

> No one can say "Jesus is Lord" except by the Holy Spirit.
>
> Now there are varieties of gifts, but the same Spirit; and there are varieties of service, but the same Lord; and there are varieties of working, but it is the same God who inspires them all in every one. To each is given the manifestation of the Spirit for the common good.
>
> For just as the body is one and has many members, and all the members of the body, though many, are one body, so it is with Christ. For by one Spirit we were all baptized into one body—Jews or Greeks, slaves or free—and all were made to drink of one Spirit.
>
> 1 Corinthians 12:3-7, 12-13

Wind and Fire

Late spring in the midwest, where I live, is a season of storms. Hot, muggy days are cooled by periodic thunderstorms. Often fierce and dramatic, these storms usually blow in on a gale of wind, darkening the sky, then treating those of us below to a show of thunder and lightning the likes of which one cannot see anywhere else. Occasionally the oncoming storms turn threatening. They can carry arsenals of hail. Lightning may strike terrifyingly close by. They can, when conditions are ripe, become tornados. The sun's light leeches out, turning the sky an eerie yellow-green, and an ominous stillness hangs in the breezeless air. Suddenly, the relentless vortex of a tornado funnel emerges whirling and plunging, gathering fierce momentum as it whips its way along its appointed path.

Generally, I view the drama of midwestern spring skies from the shelter of a kitchen or office window, but on occasion I have experienced one close at hand. I recall with special vividness the spring of 1990. I had spent the week teaching a graduate ministerial course in Sioux Falls, South Dakota. Our home in Omaha, Nebraska, is about a five-hour trip from that city, so I had driven up on Monday morning and planned to drive back home Friday afternoon following my last class. As I departed, the weather forecast was ambiguous—possible thundershowers, possible tornados. But the sky was clear. So I set off on the drive southward, planning to arrive home in time to meet my husband and children at a party at a friend's house.

The roads that run north-south in this part of the country are much more sparsely traveled and less developed than the east-west roadways. On the trek between Sioux Falls and Omaha one travels through only a few towns of any size. Sioux Falls (population 100,000) is the largest city next to Omaha (population 500,000). Sioux City is halfway between, the home of 80,000 people. Other than that, towns are small and far apart. On much of the highway one drives by open fields. There are few rest stops, only a rare gas station, a smattering of habitations. One can drive for twenty, thirty, or forty miles without finding a place to stop or even the hint of human presence.

I set out somewhat warily because I knew that I did not want to find myself alone on that desolate highway when a storm passed by. So I had my road maps and I kept my radio tuned to the local stations that kept listeners continually apprised of weather conditions. For the first hour of the drive things went well. Then I began to see stormy skies to the west of me. The radio informed me of the counties in which thunderstorm and tornado watches were in effect, and I was kept busy trying to figure out from the maps and the passing road signs which county I was presently passing through. I figured I could make it to Sioux City, about halfway between my departure point and destination, by supper time. I could stop there, and the storm in the west, which was traveling rapidly east and would no doubt meet me, could be avoided in the shelter of a restaurant. I drove quickly and reached Sioux City just in time to get seated in the cafe before the storm struck. It was impressive. When I got out of the car the wind was at gale levels and the sky to the near west was growing dark. Ten minutes later the sky covered over to pitch black. Inside the cafe, the few patrons watched with wonder as the blackness, filled with fierce, whipping wind, became a thundering waterfall. Thick sheets of rain beat relentlessly down upon the building. The parking lot, our cars, the roadside sign were invisible in the inky, rainlashed dark. I wondered if this was what it was like during the monsoon season in India, only chilly instead of tropical.

After an hour the storm passed. I waited for the sky to clear and figured I was home-free for the rest of the southward journey. All the turbulent weather seemed to have passed by, so I set out again. The road south seemed clear, and I drove for another half hour without incident. On my left the sky was alive with lightning, but I assumed that this was the same storm system that I had experienced moving east and south. I had difficulty finding a local radio station and could not yet pick up an Omaha transmission. So I simply drove.

The activity in the sky to my left increased but, I reasoned, I am headed south, straight ahead, and I shouldn't have any problems. Much to my surprise, however, the highway, which I had assumed was headed due south, suddenly curved left. I was headed right into the stormy skies. What I had thought was the east was in fact the south (the stormy weather made accurate assessment of time of day or direction difficult). I found an Omaha station and quickly learned that tornado warnings were in effect there. Tornados are no laughing matter, and one does not relish the thought of driving into the path of one.

As there was no place to stop I had no choice but to keep going, listen to the radio, and hope that my path and the storm's did not cross. I kept my eyes peeled for a bridge or a reststop or a commercial business or even a private home. There was nothing. No billboards. No road signs. No nothing.

Soon, the wind began to pick up. I was entering the edge of the storm system. The car I was driving was our around-town car, a lightweight two-door with a marginal facility for holding the road. I wanted desperately to find shelter, but there was none. The wind gained momentum and made holding the car in one lane nearly impossible. The radio announced the proximity of impending dangerous storms. I knew I needed to seek safety. I thought of abandoning the car by the side of the road and seeking shelter in the roadside ditch (a scenario suggested by safety warnings I had read), but the wind was so strong I couldn't get the fear out of my head that it would roll my car over on me or that, being the only object on the vast plain, it would attract lightning or that if a tornado indeed touched down, the car and I would be snatched up and hurled into oblivion.

Out of the darkness a lone road sign emerged: Next rest stop: five miles. I prayed hard that I could make it, the other alternatives seeming too risky, and the eye of the storm still being several miles away. With enormous difficulty I kept the wind-battered car from careening off the road and finally guided it onto the offramp where the modest concrete reststop could be seen in the near distance. I pulled in. Several other travelers had sought shelter under its eaves, and we huddled there, listening to the squawk and scratch of the weather reports. The storm finally broke just as I was phoning my family, who, it turned out, were in the basement of the friend's house, partying below ground in response to the tornado warnings.

Two hours later, the pelting rain and sky-pyrotechnics had ceased, and one by one the cars pulled out of the reststop and headed home. The sky cleared. What had seemed like midnight because of the darkness was now revealed to be a spring evening. Rosy light filtered through the dissolving clouds and laid swatches of sunlight on the wet road. The air was incredibly sweet. The calm of the evening was deliciously quiet and reassuring. Soon the sky was cloudless and translucent with shimmering, purple-tinged light. I drove home bathed in the exquisite beauty of a world made fresh and new by the passing power of wind and fire.

God's Spirit moves and breathes in creation in a thousand ways. We feel its beating in our hearts, we sense its restless motion in the visions and dreams that urge us on as Christian community. Creative, ever-animating, inspiring, goading, drawing us, we know that the Spirit is among and with us.

If the spiritual life, and God as well, is not static, is not simply homeostasis or regal presence, if God and the spiritual life are also dynamic, challenging and transforming, then perhaps the Spirit can be imaged not only as a gentle dove but as a midwestern storm. The power, awesome beauty, and utter freedom of the storm speaks to me of the power, beauty, and freedom of the Spirit of God that acts in and through our lives.

On the feast of the Spirit the church traditionally sings the Pentecost Sequence, that special ancient hymn sung before the gospel. We cry out for the descent. We long for comfort, for presence, for guidance, for empowerment. We ask for the gifts. Whether the Spirit comes as tender love on the wings of a dove or as fierce love in the rush of wind and flame, we celebrate its coming.

> *Holy Spirit, Lord Divine,*
> *Come from heights of heav'n and shine.*
> *Come with blessed radiance bright!*
>
> *Come, O Father of the poor,*
> *Come, whose treasured gifts endure.*
> *Come, our heart's unfailing light!*
>
> *Of consolers, wisest, best,*
> *And our soul's most welcome guest,*
> *Sweet refreshment, Sweet repose.*
>
> *In our labor, rest most sweet,*
> *Pleasant coolness in the heat,*
> *Consolation in our woes.*
>
> *Light most blessed, shine with grace*
> *In our heart's most secret place,*
> *Fill your faithful through and through.*
>
> *Left without your presence here,*
> *Life itself would disappear,*
> *Nothing thrives apart from you.*

Cleanse our soiled hearts from sin,
Arid souls refresh within,
Wounded lives to health restore.

Bend the stubborn heart and will,
Melt the frozen, warm the chill,
Guide the wayward home once more!

On the faithful who are true
And profess their faith in you,
In your sev'nfold gift descend!

Give us virtue's sure reward,
Give us your salvation, Lord,
Give us joys that never end![60]

Notes

1. Julian of Norwich, *A Shewing of God's Love*, edited by Sister Anna Maria Reynolds (London: Longmans, Green and Co., 1958), p. 10.

2. I especially recommend Raymond E. Brown's three books *A Crucified Christ in Holy Week: Essays on the Four Gospel Passion Narratives* (Collegeville, MN: Liturgical Press, 1986); *A Risen Christ in Eastertime: Essays on the Gospel Narratives of the Resurrection* (Collegeville, MN: Liturgical Press, 1991); and *A Once-and-Coming Spirit at Pentecost* (Collegeville, MN: Liturgical Press, 1994).

3. T.S. Eliot, *Collected Poems 1909-1962* (New York: Harcourt, Brace & World, 1970), p. 94.

4. Sallie McFague in her book *The Body of God: An Ecological Theology* (Minneapolis: Augsburg Publishers, Fortress, 1993) develops this striking idea.

5. John Climacus, *The Ladder of Divine Ascent*, translated by Colm Luibheid and Norman Russell (New York: Paulist Press, 1982), pp. 167-69.

6. *The Spiritual Exercises of St. Ignatius. A New Translation Based on Studies in the Language of the Autograph*. Louis J. Puhl (Chicago: Loyola University Press, 1951), p. 60.

7. *Ibid.*, p. 61.

8. *Ibid.*, p. 62.

9. Flannery O'Connor, *Everything that Rises Must Converge* (New York: Farrar, Straus and Giroux, 1965 edition), pp. 217-18.

10. On this social ethics tradition see Michael J. Schultheis, Edward P. DeBerri, and Peter J. Henroit, *Our Best Kept Secret: The Rich Heritage of Catholic Social Teaching* (Washington, D.C.: Center of Concern, 1987).

11. *The Gospel in Art by the Peasants of Solentiname*, edited by Philip and Sally Scharper (Maryknoll, NY: Orbis Books, 1984), p. 36.

12. Text: Claudia F. Hernaman, 1838-1898, alt. Tune: St. Flavian; John's Day Psalter, 1562; Harm based on original *faux-bourdon* setting.

13. John Donne, *Selections from Divine Poems, Sermons, Devotions and Prayers*, edited and introduced by John Booty (New York: Paulist Press, 1990), p. 106.

14. Thomas Merton, *The Wisdom of the Desert* (New York: New Directions, 1960), pp. 75-76.

15. Benedicta Ward, tr., *The Sayings of the Desert Fathers* (London: A.R. Mowbray, 1975), p. 117.

16. Text: Frederick W. Faber, 1814-1863, alt. Tune: In Babilone, 8787D; Oude en Nieuwe Hollanste Boerenlitties, c. 1710.

17. Text: Stabat Mater Dolorosa; Jacopone da Todi, 1230-1306. Tr. by Anthony G. Petti, 1932-1985, © 1971 Faber Music. Tune: Stabat Mater, 88 7; Mainz Gesangbuch, 1661; Harm. by Richard Proulx b. 1937. © 1906, GIA Publications, Inc.

18. Margaret Ebner, *Major Works*, translated by Leonard P. Hindsley (New York: Paulist Press, 1993), pp. 113-114.

19. John and Charles Wesley, *Selected Writings and Hymns*, edited and introduced by Frank Whaling (New York: Paulist Press, 1981), p. 197.

20. In the Roman Catholic Church until 1955 the fifth Sunday of Lent was known as Passion Sunday. It was suppressed as a separate observance and combined with Palm Sunday at that time. Other denominations involved in liturgical renewal have tended to follow suit, and the Sunday before Easter, while it still celebrates Jesus' entry into Jerusalem, now emphasizes the Passion narrative read from one of the Synoptic Gospels.

21. Text: Gloria, laus et honor; Theodulph of Orleans c. 760-821; Tr. by John M. Neale. 1818-1866 alt. Tune: St. Theodulph, 76760D: Melchior Teschner, 1584-1635. This hymn, whose text dates from the ninth century, is traditionally associated with this celebration.

22. Text: American folk hymn. Tune: Let Us Break Bread, 10 10 6 8 7; American folk hymn. Harm. by David Hurd, b. 1950. GIA Publications, Inc.

23. Quoted in Carolyn Walker Bynum, *Holy Feast and Holy Fast: The Religious Significance of Food to Medieval Women* (Berkeley, CA: University of California Press, 1987), p. 176.

24. That Jesus himself took on the culturally sanctioned roles usually reserved to women has been one of the new ideas given light in recent biblical scholarship. See Diane Jacobs-Malina, *Beyond Patriarchy: The Images of Family in Jesus* (New York: Paulist Press, 1993).

25. Julian of Norwich, *Showings*, translated by Edmund Colledge and James Walsh (New York: Paulist Press, 1978), p. 297.

26. *Ibid.*, pp. 297-98.

27. *The Prayers of Catherine of Siena*, edited by Suzanne Hoffke (New York: Paulist Press, 1983), pp. 172-73. The selection is from number 19, Prayer for Passion Sunday, 1379.

28. Text: Afro-American Spiritual. Tune: Were You There, 10 10 with refrain; Afro-American Spiritual; Harm. by C. Winfred Douglas, 1867-1944, © 1940, 1943, 1961, Church Pension Fund.

29. St. Athanasius described this as "The Word became [human] in order that we might be made divine." Quoted in John Breck, *The Power of the Word in the Worshiping Church* (Crestwood, New York: St. Vladimir's Seminary Press, 1986), p. 218.

30. Clement of Alexandria, *Exhortation* 10.110. Quoted in Jaroslav Pelikan, *Jesus Through the Centuries: His Place in the History of Culture* (New Haven: Yale University Press, 1985), p. 39.

31. Athanasius, *Contra Gentes* 41. Quoted in George A. Maloney, *The Cosmic Christ: From Paul to Teilhard* (New York: Sheed and Ward, 1968), p. 261.

32. The exception to this generalization can be found in Han Urs von Balthasar, *Mysterium Paschale: The Mystery of Easter*, trans. Aidan Nichols (Grand Rapids, MI: William B. Eerdmans, 1990).

33. Text: John M. C. Crum, 1872-1958, © Oxford University Press. Tune: Noël Nouvelet, 11 10 11 10, French Carol; Harm. by Thomas Foster, b. 1938, © 1986, GIA Publications, Inc.

34. *The Poems of Gerard Manley Hopkins*, edited by W. H. Gardner and N. H. MacKenzie (Oxford: Oxford University Press, 1970), pp. 34-35.

35. Brother Lawrence, *The Practice of the Presence of God: Being Conversations and Letters of Nicholas Harman of Lorraine* (Grand Rapids, MI: Fleming H. Revell Co., 1958), p. 13.

36. Text: St. I *Surrexit Christus Hodie*, Latin, 14th c.; Para. in *Lyra Davidica*, 1708, alt.; St. 2, 3, *The Compleat Psalmodist*, c. 1750, alt.; St. 4 Charles Wesley, 1707-1788. Tune: *Easter Hymn*, 77 77 with alleluias; *Lyra Davidica*, 1708.

37. Quoted in the video "The Romanian Solution," segment of *The Long Search* produced by the BBC.

38. George Herbert, *The Country Parson, The Temple*, edited by John N. Wall, Jr. (New York: Paulist Press, 1981), pp. 155-56.

39. *An Interrupted Life: The Diaries of Etty Hillesum* (New York: Pantheon Books, 1983).

40. Text: O Filii Et Filiae; Jean Tesserand, d. 1494; Tr. by John M. Neale, 1818-1866 alt. Tune: O Filii Et Filiae, 888 with alleluias; Mode II; Ac. by Richard Proulx, b. 1937, © 1975 GIA Publications.

41. Jaroslav Pelikan, *Jesus Through the Centuries: His Place in the History of Culture* (New Haven, Conn.: Yale University Press, 1985).

42. *Quaker Spirituality: Selected Writings*, edited by Douglas V. Steere (New York: Paulist Press, 1984), pp. 88-89.

43. Dorothy Day, *Meditations*, selected and arranged by Stanley Vishnewski (New York: Paulist Press, 1970), pp. 52-53.

44. "Prayer for Peace" in *Worship: A Hymnal and Service Book for Roman Catholics* (Chicago: GIA Publications, 1986), section 1193.

45. Notably the twelfth-century Cistercian Aelred of Rievaulx in his treatise *Spiritual Friendship* (Washington, D.C.: Cistercian Publications, 1974) and Francis de Sales, seventeenth-century bishop, in his *Introduction to the Devout Life* (Garden City, NY: Doubleday Image Books, 1955).

46. Ignatius of Antioch, "Letter to the Romans" in *Early Christian Fathers*, edited by Cyril C. Richardson (New York: Collier Books, 1970), p. 104.

47. Plácido Erdozaín, *Archbishop Romero: Martyr of Salvador* (Maryknoll, NY: Orbis Books, 1981), p. 75.

48. Cf. Sophia Cavalletti, *The Religious Potential of the Child* (New York: Paulist Press, 1983).

49. 23rd Psalm. Revised Standard Version.

50. *Lyric and Dramatic Poems of John G. Neihardt* (Lincoln: University of Nebraska Press, 1973), pp. 117-18.

51. Catherine of Siena, *The Dialogue*, translation by Suzanne Noffke (New York: Paulist Press, 1980), p. 12. Her friend and confessor Raymond of Capua is quoted here.

52. *Ibid.*, p. 25.

53. *Ibid.*, pp. 60-61.

54. *Ibid.*, p. 62.

55. Text: Sydney Carter, b. 1915 © Galliard Publications. Tune: Shaker Song, Irregular; American Shaker; Harm. by Sydney Carter, b. 1915 © Galliard Publications.

56. *From Glory to Glory: Texts from Gregory of Nyssa's Mystical Writings* (Crestwood, NY: *St. Vladimir's Seminary Press*, 1979), p. 29.

57. Text: Latin, 9th c.; Tr. by Richard Proulx, b. 1937 © 1975, 1986, GIA Publications, Inc. Tune: *Ubi Caritas*, 12 12 12 12 with refrains Mode VI; Acc. by Richard Proulx, b. 1937, © 1986, GIA Publications.

58. Creed of the Masai People, translated by Father Vincent Donovan, found in *Christianity Rediscovered* (Chicago, IL: Claretian Publications, 1981).

59. Text: *Veni Creator Spiritus*; Attr. to Rabanus Maurus, 776-856; Tr. by Edward Caswell, 1814-1978, alt. Tune: Lambillotte, L. M.; with repeat; Louis Lambillotte, SJ, 1796-1855; Harm. by Richard Proulx, b. 1937, © GIA Publications, Inc.

60. Sequence for Pentecost, *Veni Sancti Spiritus*. Text: 13th C. Tr. b Peter J. Scagnelli, b, 1949. Tune: Mode I. Acc. by Adriaan Engels, b. 1906.

ABOUT THE AUTHOR

WENDY M. WRIGHT is a gifted writer in the field of contemporary spirituality. Her writings can be found in *Weavings* and other leading journals of the spiritual life as well as in her previously published books. She is on the faculty at Creighton University in Omaha, Nebraska, where she lives with her husband and three children. Her first Upper Room Book, *The Vigil,* was published in 1992.